RAILWAY BYLINES
SUMMER SPECIAL No.3

Holiday pleasures, 1920s style... 0-6-0T ELLA looks after the holiday crowds on the Ravenglass & Eskdale Railway in the early 1920s. This *is* summertime; don't be misled by all those coats and hats – this is the Cumberland coast, after all! PHOTOGRAPH: LENS OF SUTTON

Editor
Martin Smith

All correspondence regarding
editorial matters should be addressed to
<u>THE EDITOR</u>
Railway Bylines Summer Special
PO Box 1957, Radstock,
Bath, BA3 5YJ
Tel. & Fax :- 01373 812048
OFFICE HOURS ONLY PLEASE
E-mail the Editor
smudger@ivycot49.freeserve.co.uk

<u>DISTRIBUTION</u>
<u>ENQUIRIES</u>
The magazine Railway Bylines is published monthly by
Irwell Press 59A, High Street, Clophill, Beds MK45 4BE
and distributed by Seymours Distribution Ltd, London.
Printed in Huddersfield by The Amadeus Press
All distribution enquiries regarding the NEWSTRADE
and
SPECIALIST BOOK and MODEL SHOPS should be
directed to Owen Eyles at the address opposite.
Copyright Irwell Press 2000.
All rights reserved.
Printed and bound in the UK by
The Amadeus Press, Bradford

Cover main photograph. Now there's seasonal... It is summertime at Lyme Regis – 14 August 1958, in fact – and one of the famous little Adams Radial Tanks has just arrived with a well patronised train from Axminster. PHOTOGRAPH: M.N.BLAND; THE TRANSPORT TREASURY

Upper cover photograph. Whittle Colliery, Northumberland. NCB No.47 at work on 31st August 1972. PHOTOGRAPH: TOM HEAVYSIDE

Rear cover. Our second 'mystery picture' – tell us where this is, and you could win a year's subscription to RAILWAY BYLINES. See the editorial box for details. PHOTOGRAPH: THE TRANSPORT TREASURY

Photograph far right. For those of you who thought that industrial railways were all grime and grease, here's a delightfully herbaceous scene on the 4ft 3in gauge Broom Bank railway which served the Smeed Dean Cement Works just to the north of Sittingbourne, Kent. Some time during the 1950s, Barclay 0-4-0ST WOULDHAM (W/No.1679 of 1920) was photographed approaching the cement works with a train of loaded clay wagons. PHOTOGRAPH: W.J.FORD

Photograph right._Branch lines R us... This view of a branch terminus is an archetypal BYLINES scene – out of the way, quiet and unhurried. But where is it? This picture is one half of our 'win a subscription' competition – if you can tell us where it is (we *do* know the answer!), look at the editorial box for details of how to enter. PHOTOGRAPH: ERIC ASHTON

CONTENTS

Editorial

Welcome to the RAILWAY BYLINES SUMMER SPECIAL No.3. As regular readers of RAILWAY BYLINES magazine will know, we always try very hard to find the best possible photographs – preferably, ones which haven't already been flogged to death in other magazines and books. But when it comes to this SUMMER SPECIAL, we must smugly admit to being rather pleased with ourselves – to the best of our knowledge, the greater proportion of the 110 photographs we have used are previously unpublished. In fact, when it came to having the prints made, some of the negatives, although forty or more years old, were being placed in an enlarger for the very first time! Photographs don't come much fresher than that!

We hope you enjoy what's on offer in this year's SUMMER SPECIAL. If you happen to be stumbling across us for the first time, remember that you can treat yourself to a regular helping of this sort of fare – branch and secondary lines, industrial railways, narrow gauge, Irish railways and the like. The regular helping comes in the form of a 56-page magazine, RAILWAY BYLINES, which is published monthly, and will cost you a measly £3.20.

Now – if you fancy getting twelve issues of RAILWAY BYLINES magazine free, gratis and for absolutely nothing, you can enter our 'spot the station' competition. Somewhere on this or the facing page is a picture of a 'mystery station', Another 'mystery station' is pictured on the back cover. Tell us which two stations we are looking at, and you could win a year's subscription to RAILWAY BYLINES magazine. Send your entry to MARTIN SMITH, RAILWAY BYLINES, PO BOX 1957, RADSTOCK, BATH BA3 5YJ to reach us by 26 October 2000 (for those of you with poor memories for dates, 26 October is, of course, Punkie Night at Hinton St.George in Somerset). All correct entries will be placed in the editor's red and white bobble hat, and the first one to be drawn will win the prize.

Even if you don't wish to enter our competition, you are most welcome to write, phone, fax or e-mail us. If you have any comments about this SUMMER SPECIAL, please get in touch – we will try to include a selection of readers' letters and comments in a forthcoming issue of RAILWAY BYLINES magazine.

Left. Opening day at Dornoch – see page 78. *(Courtesy The Scottish Record Office).*

THE GREAT EASTERN RAILWAY'S Y14 CLASS 0-6-0s
- the LNER J15s

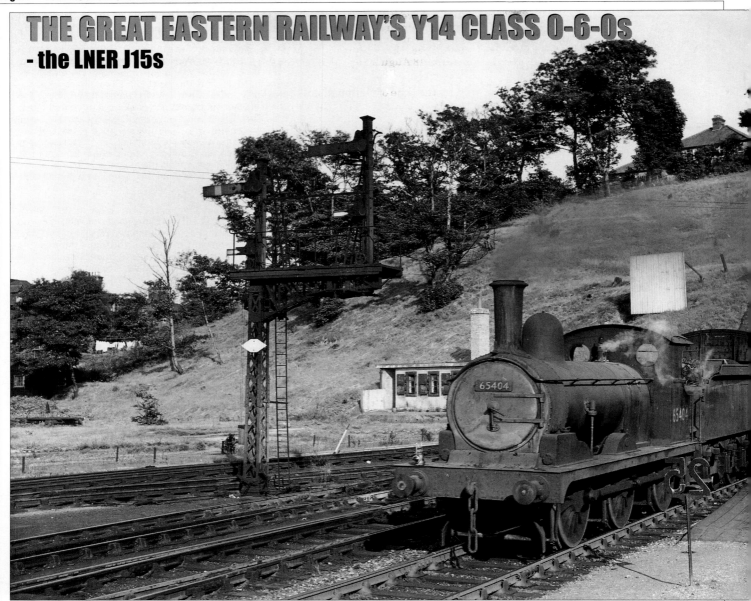

The year of 1883 proved to be memorable for the development of the goods locomotive as, within a space of just a few weeks during the summer, not one, but two, new classes of main line 0-6-0 goods engines entered traffic. These two designs were not particularly high-profile, let alone glamorous (what 19th century 0-6-0s were?) but both were immediately successful and were to become widely regarded as all-time classics. Both stood the test of time, with a combined total of over 180 still in service at the time British Railways came into existence in 1948.

The first to make its debut in 1883 came from the Swindon Works of the Great Western Railway (GWR). In May of that year, William Dean's No.2301 – the first of what was logically known as the 'Dean Goods' – was completed; construction of these locomotives continued until January 1899, by which time a total of 260 had been built.

The second class came from the Stratford Works of the Great Eastern Railway (GER). Designed by Thomas William Worsdell, the first to be delivered, No.610, emerged from Stratford in July 1883 – this locomotive was the forerunner of what eventually became the J15 class. It is this class which is our subject here.

The GER classified No.610 as Y14. This was in keeping with company practice whereby new locomotive types took their designation from the first Stratford Works order number. Construction of Y14s continued until September 1913 when No.551, the last of no less than 289 engines, was completed. During the thirty-year period of construction several modifications and improvements had been introduced, most of them by James Holden during his 22½-year tenure as Locomotive Superintendent from July 1885 to

by Bill Aves

December 1907. There were also variations on the theme – these comprised a solitary 2-cylinder compound version which was built to a special order in 1888, and eighty-one engines of a closely related design, GER Class N31 (LNER Class J14), between 1893 and 1899. There were thus no less than 371 GER 0-6-0s built to the same basic design, although the withdrawal of the less than satisfactory N31s actually commenced before the last twenty Y14s entered service.

Almost inevitably, during such a lengthy period of construction, the role of the locomotives changed – this was also the case with the GWR's 'Dean Goods'. Around the turn of the century both types were superseded on main line goods duties and, consequently, gravitated to secondary and branch lines where they were used on passenger duties as well as goods. It was, arguably, these new spheres of activity which resulted in the locomotives having such long lives – both classes had very modest axleweights and could therefore be used on some country branches where no other 0-6-0s were permitted. Indeed, it was not until the emergence of the Ivatt Class 2 2-6-0s in the late 1940s/ early 1950s that suitable replacements became available and, even then, the entire Great Eastern Section received only five of them.

The stories of the GER Y14s and the GWR 'Dean Goods' also had parallels during World War I when engines of both classes served with the Railway Operating Division of the Royal Engineers on the Western Front. And, whilst large numbers of the GWR engines were 'called up' for War Department use in World War II, it is seldom realised that two ex-LNER J15s were also taken over by the WD.

Built as Great Eastern Railway No.910 in November 1891, No.65404 was one of the many steam-braked engines which ended its days at Ipswich, having been transferred from Norwich in November 1951. This small, simple but effective locomotive is seen here entering Ipswich station with a down local goods in high summer, on 18 August 1953. PHOTOGRAPH: J.ROBERTSON; THE TRANSPORT TREASURY

By the time of Nationalisation in 1948 the 'Dean Goods' and J15s were still well represented, but by this time each of the two types trod rather different ground – the 'Dean Goods' were used almost exclusively on branch lines and very rarely visited London, but there were still numerous J15s allocated to Stratford, the centre of the still extensive ex-GER network in London. When the last 'Dean Goods', No.2538, was withdrawn from service in May 1957, there were still fifty-three J15s in British Railways stock and another in industrial use. The last four J15s, BR Nos.65361, 65462, 65464 and 65465, were withdrawn in September 1962 – the 'last shed' for all four was Stratford.

The 'Dean Goods' rightly have their many admirers, but it is only fair to give due credit to the equally useful, but less well publicised Worsdell/Holden 0-6-0s. We are fortunate to have an example of each in preservation: GWR No.2516 at Swindon and GER No.564 (LNER No.7564/5462, BR No.65462) on the North Norfolk Railway. The latter is due to return to duty on the North Norfolk later this year (2000) following a major overhaul.

Y14s – genesis and development

Prior to taking over as the GER's Locomotive Superintendent at the beginning of 1882, T.W.Worsdell had worked for the London & North Western Railway – he had been the Works Manager at Crewe, under the legendary Francis Webb. When Worsdell joined the GER, the GNR/GER Joint Line had just been completed, allowing through working from Doncaster via Lincoln and March to the Lea Valley and Stratford. This route generated a large volume of coal traffic for industries and domestic hearths in London's East End – Yorkshire coal had hitherto been routed via the Great Northern as far as Peterborough, but could now be conveyed via the new line direct to London.

The GER was faced with an urgent need for locomotives to deal with this traffic. At the time, the mainstay of GER goods power comprised 110 of Samuel Johnson's 417 and 477 class 0-6-0s which had been built between 1867 and 1873, fifteen of William Adams unsatisfactory (and, as it turned out, short-lived) 2-6-0s of 1878, and ten Massey Bromley 552 Class 0-6-0s of 1882. These were supplemented by Adams 'Ironclad' 4-4-0s and the much older Sinclair 2-4-0s, but both types had 6ft 1in driving wheels and were, therefore, better suited to mixed traffic than heavy goods. These various types were inadequate to meet traffic requirements and so, early in 1883, the GER was even obliged to draft in a number of Adams 61 Class suburban 0-4-4Ts on the Peterborough (East)-London route. These 0-4-4Ts proved well capable of handling twenty-five loaded coal wagons, but they need six water stops *en route*!

The standard Y14s

The bottom line was that the GER needed a brand new type of goods locomotive, and T.W Worsdell's solution to the problem was a new class of 0-6-0 tender engines. These were the Y14s. As mentioned earlier, the first of the class was completed at Stratford Works in July 1883; a total

GER No.38 was one of the early Y14s, the second of an order of nineteen built by Sharp, Stewart in 1884. At the time of the Grouping in 1923 it was an Ipswich engine. It was duplicated as LNER No.07038, its former number being made available for a new J68 0-6-0T. Neither the date nor the location of this photograph are recorded, but the neat coal stacks were a feature of many Great Eastern sheds. PHOTOGRAPH: ERIC ASHTON COLLECTION

GER Y14 0-6-0s – sequence of construction

Brakes: **S** – steam; **W** – Westinghouse; **V** – vacuum ejectors
Boilers: **LG** – level grate; **SG** – sloping grate

GER Nos.	Total	Stratford Order No.	Dates built	Brakes (as built)	Boiler (as built)	Notes
610-619	10	Y14	7.83-10.83	S	LG	
620-639	10	K15	3.84-8.84	S	LG	
37-41, 119-124, 592-599	19	Built by Sharp Stewart *	4.84-7.84	S	LG	(a)
680-689	10	N16	2.85	S	LG	
690-699	10	P17	11.85-3.86	S	LG	(b)
800-809	10	M18	4.86-8.86	S	LG	(c)
810-819	10	X18	11.86-2.87	S	LG	
820-829	10	D20	9.87	S	LG	
527-536	10	U20	10.87-1.88	S	LG	
537-541, 830-834	10	R21	10.88	S	LG	
835-844	10	T22	7.89	S	LG	
845-854	10	R23	10.89	S	LG	
855-864	10	T23	10.89-11.89	S	LG	
865-874	10	Y23	11.89-12.89	S	LG	
875-884	10	U25	8.90-9.90	S	LG	
885-894	10	Y25	10.90-11.90	S	LG	
895-904	10	L28	9.91-10.91	S	SG	
905-914	10	N28	10.91-11.91	S	SG	
915-924	10	P28	11.91-12.91	S	SG	
925-934	10	S28	12.91-1.92	S	SG	
936-945	10	X28	8.92-11.92	S	SG	
Construction of Y14s halted; eighty-one N31 class 0-6-0s built 1893-98						
507-516	10	I45	5.99-6.99	S	SG	
517-526	10	S45	6.99-10.99	S	SG	
640-644	5	X45	7.99	W + VE	SG	(e)
645-649	5	X45	8.99-9.99	W	SG	(e)
552-561	10	A60	5.06-7.06	W + VE	SG	(e)
562-571	10	B70	2.12-5.12	W + VE	SG	(d)
542-551	10	G73	6.13-9.13	W + VE	SG	(d)

* Sharp Stewart locos built as the maker's W/Nos.3146-3164

(a)   No.41 became No.600 in 7.12
(b)   No.696 fitted with Joy's valve gear until 1.97
(c)   No.800 became No.609 in 1.92
(d)   Steam heating from new
(e)   Steam heating fitted 1913

of forty-nine had been built by the end of August 1884 – of these, nineteen were constructed by Sharp, Stewart & Co of Glasgow. These were the last GER locomotives from an outside locomotive manufacturer until William Beardmore & Co, also of Glasgow, supplied twenty

1500 (S69) 4-6-0s in 1920-21. The first Y14s were used on the coal traffic, and the majority of the class were still at March shed until the emergence of larger 0-6-0s (the Holden F48 and G58 – later LNER J16 and J17 classes) from 1900 onwards.

The Y14s were a straightforward design with 17½" x 24" cylinders, Stephenson link motion, slide valves, and 4ft 10in diameter wheels (later 4ft 11in with thicker tyres), the diameter which became standard for all subsequent classes of GER 0-6-0 tender engines.

Worsdell stayed at Stratford only until July 1885, when he left to take up a more remunerative position with the North Eastern Railway at their Gateshead Works. One of Worsdell's early designs for the NER was the C Class 0-6-0 (LNER J21 class) which, like their GER counterparts, was also destined to be very numerous, no less than 201 being built by the end of 1895. However, most of these NER engines entered service as 2-cylinder compounds and, as will be seen from the accompanying table, were considerably heavier than his Great Eastern locomotives.

Worsdell's successor at Stratford was James Holden, who had latterly been employed by the GWR at Swindon Works. Holden was clearly well satisfied with his predecessor's design, not least because it fitted in with his own ideas on standardisation, and so construction of the Y14s continued. By 1893, the remarkable total of 229 were in service. In the meantime, though, several variants had been tried.

Joy's valve gear

The M15 class 2-4-2Ts which Worsdell had designed for the GER's London suburban services had proved disappointing, having rapidly earned a reputation for being heavy on coal and for being sluggish and unpredictable on the road. At the time, this had been attributed to the difficulty of setting their Joy's valve gear accurately (although recent research has indicated that the GER drivers' 'full regulator' technique was largely responsible for the lo-

No.7592 was yet another Ipswich engine, and is seen at its home shed early in the LNER era. It sports the grey livery which had been adopted by the GER towards the end of the Great War, and was still used by Stratford for several years after the Grouping. It retains the stovepipe chimney, low pitched wooden-roofed cab and Ramsbottom safety valves, and has the most common type of tender with its unequal wheelbase and 'D'-frame slots. No.7592 was another of the Sharp, Stewart order, and was withdrawn in 1928. PHOTOGRAPH: THE TRANSPORT TREASURY

No.7521 was one of the last order for steam-braked Y14s, and was built at Stratford in June 1899. It was one of the final withdrawals (from Cambridge shed) before the outbreak of war in September 1939 brought a halt to the scrapping process. In this picture, which can be dated to the mid-1930s, it is in its original condition except for the replacement 'Darlington-style' chimney. Note that, unlike many of the later members of the class which ran, from new, with second-hand tenders, it is coupled to one of the post-1892 series with 'sausage-shaped' frame slots. PHOTOGRAPH: W.HERMISTON; THE TRANSPORT TREASURY

comotives' perceived shortcomings). In order to find out more about the Joy's valve gear and its possible failings, in the latter part of 1885 James Holden experimentally fitted Y14 No.696 (which was then under construction at Stratford), not only with the Joy's motion, but also a pair of 18in cylinders which had been intended for a new 2-4-2T, No.674. The 2-4-2T, in turn, took the smaller cylinders and Stephenson's link motion which had been destined for the Y14. To accommodate the valve chests above the cylinders of No.696, the boiler was pitched 7½in higher than normal. The results of the exchange were entirely predictable – the economy of the 2-4-2T was much improved, but that of the goods engine was inferior to the rest of its class. Nevertheless, No.696 ran in this condition until January 1897 when it was fitted with Stephenson's motion and was given new cylinders, thus becoming a 'standard' Y14.

The compound 0-6-0
The designer of the Y14s, T.W.Worsdell, had been attracted to the principle of compounding and, during his incumbency at Stratford, had introduced a class of eleven 4-4-0s which used his version of the von Borries system. Early in 1888, James Holden also built a 2-cylinder compound. This was No.127, an 0-6-0 with cylinders of 18in x 24in high pressure and a 26in x 24in low pressure cylinder. The boiler was pitched at 7ft 6in but, otherwise, its principal dimensions were similar to the Y14s. Interestingly, the locomotive's numberplate included the inscription 'Compound No.12', and a plate on the central splasher carried the Worsdell-von Borries patent licence number. No.127 was au-

thorised as 'D&P 203' under the Stratford Works 'Departmental and Personal' series instead of a conventional Order Number, so that its costs were recorded in detail. During 1890 it was involved in trials with standard Y14s Nos.815 and 874; the trials also examined the consequences of variations in boiler pressures and cylinder diameter. No.127 was renumbered as No.935 in July 1891, and was eventually rebuilt and assimilated into Class N31 in July 1895.

Boiler modifications
Over the years there were several changes in the detail design of the 4ft 4in diameter boilers fitted, not only to the Y14s, but also a number of other GER classes. However, the boilers were broadly of two types. The earlier version was used on all engines built up to the end of 1890 (the last being Nos.885-94 of Order Number Y25); it had a level grate and had the dome on the middle of three rings. The same design of boiler was also used on the first fifty T19 Class 7ft 2-4-0s.

In April 1890, a revised design with a 1 in 12 sloping grate was introduced on T19 No.760. This type of boiler was subsequently used for the Y14s, the first batch to be thus fitted being Nos.895-904 (Order L28), built in September/October 1891. Starting with No.925 (Order S28) which was completed in December 1891, the boilers were further modified, being constructed in two rings with the dome on the front ring.

The earlier engines built with a level ('square bottom' – LNER Diagram 31) grate could not use the later sloping ('bevel bottom' – LNER Diagram 32) firebox boilers as there were differences in the rear

framing. However, it was possible for the later engines to be fitted with the older type of boilers. Replacement 'old-style' Diagram 31 boilers, also of the two-ring type, were built at Stratford up to 1928, but from 1932 the frames of a number of the earlier engines were modified to accept the sloping grate of the Diagram 32 boilers. Ross 'Pop' safety valves were fitted by the LNER – most of the surviving members of the class had been thus fitted by the time of Nationalisation, but No.5380 (formerly No.7872), for example, which was sent to Darlington to be scrapped in January 1948, retained the cased Ramsbottom type until the end.

The 'N31' hiatus
In his T19 class 7ft express passenger 2-4-0s of 1886, James Holden placed the valve chests below, instead of between, the cylinders as on the Y14s. This layout was followed on the D27 class 2-2-2s and T26 class 'Intermediate' 2-4-0s (LNER class E4). In his quest for greater standardisation, Holden eventually applied the same principle to the original Y14 design, and the first locomotive to be constructed to the revised configuration was No.999, built to Order Number N31 in January 1893. Over the next six years a further eighty engines were built to the revised design; the experimental compound, No.127, was also rebuilt to the new design.

These new N31 class 0-6-0s had their boilers pitched at 7ft 6in to correspond with other standard Holden designs, with the result that they looked much more powerful than their predecessors. But appearances were deceptive! On 0-6-0s, the leading axle was the same height in

GER No.547 was one of the very last order of 'Little Goods', being built in July 1913. It was intended from the outset to be a mixed traffic engine, hence the dual brakes. After the Grouping it duly became LNER No.7547; behind it in this picture is No.7910, a steam-braked J15. Both engines retain their cased Ramsbottom safety valves, with the whistle mounted alongside. This picture was taken in the late 1930s, probably at Colchester. PHOTOGRAPH: J.T.RUTHERFORD; THE TRANSPORT TREASURY

the frames as the driving axle and so the valve rod was inclined downwards to pass under the former. However, on the N31s the steam chests were so low in the frames that they acted as a condenser! The tortuous steam passages resulted in the cylinders and valves becoming water-logged, priming, and tardy and irregular reactions to movements of the regulator.

The N31s were certainly not one of life's success stories – on account of their dismal performance they were sarcastically known as 'Swifts' or 'Waterburies' (the name of a cheap make of watch) – and withdrawal commenced as early as 1908. Only eighteen of the eighty-two survived to become LNER Class J14. None lasted long enough to have its designated LNER '7XXX' series number applied, and the class was extinct by the end of April 1925.

The Y14 revival

In 1899, in response to the ongoing requirement for even more new freight locomotives, James Holden resumed building 'standard' Y14s which, by this time, were often referred to as the 'Little Goods'. The first two new orders, each for ten locomotives, were for engines with steam brakes only, but the third order was for five engines, Nos.640-644, to be dual-fitted (Westinghouse and vacuum) and another five, Nos.645-649, to have the Westinghouse brake only. (It should be noted that these were not the first Holden 0-6-0s to be equipped with train brakes – twenty of the ill-starred N31s built in 1894/96 had also been dual- or Westinghouse-fitted). The 'Westinghouse-only' Y14s later became LNER Nos.7645-7649, and in 1931-32 were fitted with vacuum ejectors as well.

The 'fitted' engines were intended for a variety of mixed traffic duties. As well as being used on some of the more lightly laid country branches, they were frequently employed on the burgeoning excursion traffic to the Essex Coast resorts, particularly from Liverpool Street to Southend, and including through trains from the Great Northern.

Further batches of dual-fitted Y14s were built in 1906, 1912 and 1913. This demonstrated the continuing usefulness and versatility of the design, as more modern types of 0-6-0s (F48, G58 and E72 classes – later LNER J16, J17 and J18) had, by then, entered traffic in significant numbers. The last batches of Y14s – those built in 1912 and 1913 – were fitted with steam heating from new. Later, the 1899 and 1906 engines were similarly equipped; this emphasised the class's role in the sphere of passenger work.

Renumberings

A handful of the Y14s were renumbered as follows:
• No.800 of April 1886 became No.609 in January 1892; this was a knock-on effect – No.790 was required for a new T19 2-4-0, and the M15 2-4-2T with that number became No.800.
• No.41, a Sharp Stewart-built engine of April 1884, became No.600 in April 1912, its former number going to the first of the new C72(LNER Class J68) 0-6-0Ts.
• Just after the Grouping, Nos.38 and 39 became LNER Nos.07038 and 07039; this was because of the building of additional J68 0-6-0Ts.

One of the Y14's, No.513, was withdrawn in 1920 after returning, badly damaged, from service with the Railway Operating Division in France (see below), but

Comparative dimensions of early Worsdell 0-6-0s
Dimensions are those quoted by the LNER in 1923

	J15 (GER class 'N31')	J14 (GER class 'Y14')	J21 (NER class 'C') ‡
Cylinders	2 (o) 17½" x 24"	2 (o) 17½" x 24"	2 (o) 19" x 24"
Valve gear	Stephenson and slide valves	Stephenson and slide valves	Stephenson and piston valves
Wheels	4' 11"	4' 11"	5' 1¾"
Wheelbase	7' 7" + 8' 6" = 16' 1"	7' 7" + 8' 6" = 16' 1"	8' 0" + 8' 6" = 16' 6"
Length over buffers	47' 3"	47' 3"	50' 8¼"
Boiler – diameter	4' 4"	4' 4"	4' 3"
– pitch	6' 10½"	7' 6"	7' 5½"
Total heating surfaces	1164.7 sqft	1164.7 sqft	1133.0 sqft
Grate area	18.0 sqft	18.0 sqft	17.2 sqft
Boiler pressure	160 psi	160 psi	160 psi
Tractive effort (@ 85%)	16,942lb	16,942lb	19,237lb
Weight (working order)	37 tons 2 cwt	38 tons 19 cwt	42 tons 8 cwt
Max. axle load	13 tons 10 cwt	14 tons 8 cwt	15 tons 10 cwt
Water capacity *	2,640 galls	2,640 galls	3,038 galls
Coal capacity *	5 tons	5 tons	5 tons
BR Power/route class	2F; RA1	-	2F; RA3

* GER 0-6-0s used a variety of tenders; the figures quoted are for the most common type.
‡ NER 'C' class introduced 1886. Of the 201 locos built, 171 were originally 2-cylinder compounds but were rebuilt as simples by the end of 1913. A number were superheated from 1914, but the boiler dimensions quoted are for the most common saturated type.

withdrawal of the class did not begin in earnest until 1922 when sixteen went for scrap – these included some Holden engines built as recently as 1890. Under LNER auspices the Y14s were classified J15 and, in common with all ex-GER engines, had 7000 added to their numbers, although six of the class were withdrawn before they had had their '7XXX' numbers applied. During the 1920s and 1930s withdrawals continued steadily and, by the end of 1939, only 130 of the original 289 remained. Somewhat inevitably, there were no withdrawals during World War II when there was work for almost any locomotive, no matter how elderly or infirm. However, withdrawals recommenced in 1947. By this time the survivors had been renumbered in the 5350-5479 sequence; this was part of Edward Thompson's wholesale renumbering of LNER locomotives.

A total of 127 J15s were taken into British Railways stock on 1 January 1948, but fifty-six of these were withdrawn without having had their new five-digit (6XXXX) numbers applied. By the end of 1952 the ranks had been reduced to just sixty-two by the withdrawal of most of the steam-braked goods engines. The locomotives' post-war history is shown in the accompanying table.

Details and modifications
Cabs and tender cabs: The Y14s built from 1899 onwards had noticeably shallower cab-side cut-outs.

Great Eastern locomotives of the Worsdell and Holden eras were built with wooden cab roofs. Under the LNER, from the early 1930s these were replaced by

higher-pitched steel roofs, and by the end of that decade all the surviving J15s in service had been thus altered. Additionally, in 1934/35 five of the seven steam-braked engines which had been given vacuum ejectors for passenger work were also fitted with side-window cabs and tender-back cabs for working the Colne Valley line, which had no turntables and, therefore, required much tender-first work. The locomotives concerned were Nos.7512, 7523, 7888, 7911 and 7941 (later BR Nos.65432, 65438, 65391, 65405 and 65424 respectively), which thereafter spent most of their time at either Cambridge or Colchester shed.

Many of the J15s were latterly employed on other branch lines on which there was also regular tender-first working, and these engines also ran with tender cabs or weatherboards. Some of the tender cabs were quite elaborate, being constructed from the backs of cabs of withdrawn tank engines, but others, extemporised locally at the country sheds in East Anglia, were more rudimentary. The tenders which had a form of protection often found their way from engine to engine, as required.

Tenders: Although some of the Worsdell and Holden 0-6-0s (of various classes) entered traffic with second-hand tenders, most engines were paired with tenders of the design which was standard at the time of their construction. The type in use from 1883 to 1889 – i.e. those which were attached to the first 130 of the Y14s – had an unequal wheelbase of 6ft 6in + 5ft 6in and had a capacity of 2,755 gallons of water and 5 tons of coal; the coal space had a 'self-trimming' sloping bot-

tom. Starting with Nos.845-854 (Order R23, delivered in October 1889), the tenders are externally similar to the earlier ones but, internally, had a rectangular, flat-bottomed coalbox with a reduced water capacity of 2,640 gallons. All these tenders had 'D'-shaped frame slots, but in 1892 elongated, 'sausage-shaped' slots were first seen; these were used on new tenders of this series. It is of interest that the tender of the preserved J15, ex-GER No.564 of 1912, has 'D' slots and a rectangular coalbox – these features date its construction to some time between 1889 and 1892, i.e. more than 20 years earlier than the engine itself.

The first of the 'passenger' Y14s, Nos.640-649 of 1899, were paired with larger 3,066-gallon Worsdell tenders which had previously been used by his G14 2-4-0s of 1883. (Five of the original Worsdell Y14s, Nos.615-19, had also been paired with this type when new). These tenders were similar to the normal ones, but were readily distinguishable by their side-sheets being six inches higher. The large tenders were gradually replaced, but in 1949 J15 No.65442 (one-time GER No.642) of Bury St.Edmunds shed was still paired with one of this design. At about the same time, No.65384 (GER No.877), a steam-braked engine shedded at Colchester, was also running with a similar large tender, but this is believed to have been even older, and to have come from one of Massey Bromley's 7ft 6in 4-2-2s of 1879/82.

One other type of tender appeared behind some J15s in the 1940s and early 1950s. This was the Holden-designed round-topped 2,790-gallon 'Watercart'

This superb period piece shows a dual-braked J15, believed to be No.7552, shunting the goods yard alongside the station at Hunstanton in 1928. Under the footbridge is a delightful selection of Great Eastern signals; the lower quadrant starting signals are hidden from view, but the small 'shallow X' shaped arms are 'calling on' signals, and below them are shunting signals with rings on their arms. PHOTOGRAPH: J.A.C.KIRKE; THE TRANSPORT TREASURY

In June 1932, No.7888 was equipped with the vacuum brake, and just over two years later in August 1934 was one of five members of the class to be given a new single side-window cab and a back cab, principally for working along the Colne Valley line. It is seen here on 20 May 1957 at its home shed, Cambridge, as No.65391; by this time it had acquired a medium length chimney. Note the Class E4 2-4-0 in the background. PHOTOGRAPH: R.C.RILEY

which had originally been built for his oil-fired P43 class 4-2-2s of 1898 – this type of tender had also been used by some of the T19 and T26 2-4-0s and the early 'Claud Hamilton' 4-4-0s. The J15s noted with these 'Watercart' tenders in late LNER days were Nos.5447 and 5462 while, in BR days, Nos.65451 and 65456 ran with these tenders. No.65447 (former LNER No.5447) reappeared with a

'Watercart' *circa* 1952. It seems that, in the case of the J15s, the 'Watercarts' were used only briefly after visits to Stratford Works when their 'own' tenders had been detained for repairs.

But not everything about the J15s' tenders is crystal clear. There is a photograph on the rear cover of the *Railway Bylines Summer Special No.2* of a J15, believed to be No.65462, heading a train of fish

vans at Lowestoft in the 1950s. Its tender – with 'D' slots – is unmistakably fitted with a tablet exchanger. Although several J15s spent very short periods at ex-Midland & Great Northern sheds in the late 1940s, none is known to have had a tablet exchanger. We know that No.(6)5462 was shedded at Lowestoft from November 1947 until July 1960, but there was no obvious reason why an en-

No.65457 was ex-works from Stratford in March 1958, but looks in a disreputable state in Cambridge shed yard on 9 September 1959. The tender cab, unlike those specially made in the mid-1930s for the five vacuum-fitted engines, is one of those apparently conjured up from parts of the cabs of scrapped ex-GER 2-4-2Ts. PHOTOGRAPH: PETER GROOM

gine from that shed should require a tablet exchanger.

Chimneys: All the Y14s were built with the contemporary GER stovepipe with a beaded rim. During the 1930s, these were replaced by Darlington-designed cast iron chimneys. However, during World War II plain stovepipes appeared on some J15s while other members of the class were fitted with much shorter-rimmed chimneys to enable them to work over London Transport lines which had restricted clearances. While the tall-rimmed chimney remained by far the most common type, some engines carried a medium-height chimney. In May 1960 No.65469 and 65471 were given replica GER stovepipes at Norwich shed, that on the latter being subsequently passed to No.65462 which was saved for preservation.

In the 1940s several J15s shedded at Bury St.Edmunds were fitted with stovepipe chimneys and external spark arresters for shunting at the Barnham ammunition depot on the Thetford branch. Of these engines, No.7932 (BR No.65420) retained its arrester, latterly attached to a medium-length chimney, into the mid-1950s.

Snowploughs: Nos.65370 and 65361 were noted on Stratford shed in January 1956 and March 1958 respectively with a small Cowlairs-designed buffer beam-mounted snowplough. This fitting had necessitated the removal of the front buffers. According to the RCTS *'Green Guide'*, a number of other J15s – mainly steam-braked engines – had their front buffer beams drilled to take these ploughs, and were, no doubt, used on snowplough duties at other sheds in the exposed open spaces of East Anglia.

Trip-cock gear: In the early years of World War II, twelve dual-fitted J15s were given trip-cock apparatus in case they had to be used in an emergency on London Transport electrified lines. This equipment was a standard LT fitting – it was activated by a signal at danger and released compressed air from the train pipe so that the brakes were immediately applied. On the J15s, one train-stop was fitted to the right-hand front guard iron, and the other to the left-hand rear of the tender. (The engines concerned are identified in the accompanying table). With the extension of the Central Line after the War, trip-cock equipment was retained in a modified form, and four more of the J15s were similarly fitted. The trip-cock fitted engines were intended principally for working local goods traffic between Stratford, Epping and Ongar, and on to the Fairlop Loop; consequently, most of these locomotives were allocated to Stratford District sheds. A seventeeth J15, No.65462, was also belatedly given trip-cock gear in 1961 after its transfer from Norwich to Stratford. This insignificant modification undoubtedly ensured the continued presence of so many of these small ex-GER engines in the London area throughout the 1950s.

No.930
Over the years, several railway workshops made attempts to create a record for the rapid construction of one of their locomo-

tives. In February 1878 Crewe Works completed a Webb 0-6-0 'Coal Engine', L&NWR No.1140, in 25½ hours, but in June 1888 the Pennsylvania Railroad beat this achievement hands down by building a locomotive in just 16¼ hours. Stratford Works challenged the record on 10 December 1891; the events of that day were described by C.Langley Aldrich in his *Great Eastern Locomotives Past and Present* (self-published in 1944):

'Zero hour was 9am, and 137 men and boys were detailed for the job of completing the engine and tender ready for the road. All the parts necessary had been brought to the point of assembly and methodically laid out so as to cause no hitch. They had not been previously massed nor had any attempt been made to fit them together. The gang worked furiously and the engine and tender, having also received one coat of protective "shop grey" paint, were ready for the road in 9 hours and 47 minutes from the time of starting. The boiler was filled, also the tender, and the fire laid before she came out of the shop. Following the usual weighings and adjustments, she was handed over immediately to the Running Department, completed her trial trip of 30 miles and then put into regular service hauling coal trains of 560 tons between Peterborough and London. She ran no less than 36,000 miles before she received her final coat of paint'. The record-breaking engine was No.930 of Order No.S28; she became LNER No.7930 and was withdrawn in January 1935.

Two in trouble
At 8.45am on 25 September 1900, No.522, which been completed at Stratford only one year earlier, was standing at the down home signal at Westerfield (the first station out of Ipswich on the East Suffolk line) waiting for a clear road, at the head of the Felixstowe branch goods train comprising thirty-four wagons and two brake vans, when the firebox exploded with great violence. The driver and fireman were killed. The boiler was lifted out of the engine and landed some 130 feet away but, apart from the engine itself, there was remarkably little damage. The accident was routinely investigated by the Board of Trade; the investigating officer was Lt-Col.P.G. von Donop who, in his official report, concurred with expert evidence that *'...the explosion was due to the defective attachment of the copper plate to a group of stays on the left side of the firebox, where a previous bulge had existed. The latter was situated in the vicinity of the fire and covered an area of upwards of 1½ sq.ft. Eventually the firebox at this part became too weak to sustain the working pressure in the boiler, and when the copper plate separated from the stays, the rupture followed as a natural consequence'.* No.522 was an Ipswich engine, having run 31,287 miles from new. It had apparently had no problems until June 1900 but, from then on, the drivers' report book contained no less than sixty instances of leakages in its firebox; a number of ineffective repairs had been carried out, including a temporary job at Norwich only a week earlier, sufficient to get No.522 home to Ipswich.The Board of Trade report ruled

out a boiler explosion as the safety valves were found to be in proper order; indeed, No.522 had been blowing off before the accident, and there was no shortage of water. The type of stays and the method of attaching them to the firebox had caused its rupture, and the report pointedly opined that *'...it would be well if the inspection and repairing of boilers in the Ipswich sub-division were put in the charge of an intelligent inspector...'.*

A far less dramatic event took place at Cambridge in September 1936 when J15 No.7851 was in collision with the LMSR's Kirtley 6ft 8in 2-4-0 No.20115 of Kettering shed. The damage to the J15 was clearly sufficient to warrant its withdrawal, this being effected in the following month. The Kirtley 2-4-0 did not last long either, being formally withdrawn early the following year; in all probability it had not run since the accident. The aggregate age of the two locomotives was almost 110 years, and so their demise was perhaps hardly surprising. The actual nature of the accident remains a mystery (to us, at least!); does any reader have any information as to what occurred?

War Service, 1917-19
The Great Eastern Railway made a substantial contribution to the Railway Operating Division's effort on the Western Front, no less than forty-three steam-braked Y14s being sent to France. Prior to their enlistment they were overhauled at Stratford; a number were given new boilers and/or cylinders, and there was some exchanging of tenders, no doubt to ensure that all were coupled to the standard type. They were fitted with strengthened buffer beams and side chains, and were equipped with 'White's Water Lifting Gear', to enable them to take on water from any available source such as streams and ditches.

The first thirty-six were sent in March and April 1917. These engines were:
Nos. 508, 510, 513, 517, 518, 522, 531, 532, 533, 534, 539, 616, 690, 810, 817, 826, 847, 848, 849, 856, 857, 869, 872, 887, 892, 894, 904, 911, 918, 920, 921, 925, 926, 927, 928, 940.
Seven more followed at the end of September:
Nos.507, 695, 818, 841, 876, 893, 916.

The Y14s proved popular in France – they were simple, reliable and capable of very heavy work when necessary. Although there were reported sightings of Y14s throughout the British sector of the Front, most of the engines seem to have worked between St.Pol, Doullens and Arras, and on the military lines east of Bapaume around the Canal du Nord. No.513 came to grief while working with the ROD, and was noted laid aside, with severe front end damage, at Tachincourt in January 1919. Although No.513 was repatriated with the others, its condition was so bad that it did not re-enter traffic; it was scrapped in August 1920, thereby claiming the dubious distinction of being the first of the class to be disposed of.

Sales and war service, 1942-43
Nos.7835 and 7541 were withdrawn in September 1936 but, instead of going for

scrap, were sold to London Film Productions of Denham for use in a film entitled *Knight Without Armour*. The film starred those well-known railway enthusiasts Marlene Dietrich, Robert Donat, Jacques Feyder, Irene Vanbrugh, Herbert Lomas, David Tree and Miles Malleson; the two J15s masqueraded as Russian locomotives. *Halliwell's*, incidentally, describes the film as a 'sumptuous production with charismatic stars', but does not comment on the J15s' performances.

After their cinematic exploits, the two J15s remained intact, and some five years later – in July 1942 – were overhauled at Stratford and taken over by the War Department as WD Nos.212 and 221 respectively. (The whereabouts of the two locomotives between filming in 1937 and resurrection in 1942 seem to have gone unrecorded. Does any reader know what they did or where they were kept?). The WD dispatched the two J15s to the Shropshire & Montgomeryshire Railway. No.212 was noted in the GWR's Stafford Road Works in October 1942, but in July the following year it was involved in a serious head-on collision with WD No.176 (ex-GWR 'Dean Goods' No.2558) between Shrawardine and Ford Quarry on the S&M line. Both engines were scrapped as a result. The other WD J15, No.221, remained active on the S&M until the summer of 1944, but returned to Stratford that autumn for breaking up.

A third J15 was sold out of LNER service. This was LNER No.7690 which, prior to its sale in June 1938, had been the oldest J15 – the last true Worsdell member of the class – in service. The purchaser was the Scottish Iron & Steel Company (which became part of Bairds & Scottish Steel in 1939) who put the locomotive to

work at their Gartsherrie Ironworks at Coatbridge in Lanarkshire. Designated No.1 in the ironworks fleet, it was overhauled by the Yorkshire Engine Company of Sheffield in 1952, and made several visits to Cowlairs Works, the last in July 1957. It had been fitted with a steel cab roof and 'Darlington' chimney by the LNER but, at Gartsherrie, it latterly ran with a stovepipe and a brass dome cover. It was always kept in sparkling condition by its new owner. It finished work at Gartsherrie in 1958, and is believed to have been scrapped in December of that year.

The last fifteen years – 1947 to 1962

As noted earlier, withdrawal of older steam-brake J15s continued steadily during the 1920s and 1930s but ceased with the outbreak of war in 1939. There were no further withdrawals until 1947 (by which time all 130 survivors had received their new 1946 numbers), when three Norwich engines, Nos.5358, 5369 and 5403, were taken out of service. This left eighty steam-brake and forty-seven fitted (i.e. mixed traffic) J15s to be taken into British Railways stock in 1948. By the end of 1952, sixty-five more of the steam-brake engines had gone, but there was then a pause until 1955 when Nos.65359 of King's Lynn, 65384 of Stratford and 65422 of March were scrapped. Six more went in 1956. It was not until April 1957 that the first vacuum-fitted engine, No.65356 of March, was withdrawn, but this was the only withdrawal of the year. However, from the beginning of 1958 the withdrawal of the remaining fifty-two J15s began in earnest, though some of the class continued to be repaired at Stratford – for example, Nos.65464 and

65476 were reported to be ex-works as late as October 1961.

We shall now look at the duties undertaken by these small 0-6-0s during the class's last fifteen years. The following is based largely on contemporary reports in magazines such as the *Railway Observer*, articles and correspondence in the Journal of the *Great Eastern Journal* (the magazine of the Great Eastern Railway Society) and photographic evidence, and is illustrative rather than exhaustive.

Until the end of the 1950s, J15s could be found almost anywhere on the old Great Eastern system. Because of their 'Route Availability 1' category they were often the only engines permitted on certain branch lines, but many sheds were in the habit of keeping a fitted J15 as a spare engine and so they sometimes materialised in unexpected places, on unlikely duties.

..........ooooo0OOooooo..........

STRATFORD (30A): At the time of the Grouping in 1923 almost one hundred of the class had been allocated to Stratford, but by the start of 1947 the shed's allocation had shrunk to thirty-three. Nevertheless, it was the largest allocation of J15s on the Great Eastern Section, a distinction retained until the end. A number of the class had long been sub-shedded at Ilford, Epping, Hertford (East) and Wickford, but by the BR era only Epping seems to have had a regular allocation. In addition to its own engines, Stratford shed frequently made use of visiting J15s which were running in after receiving attention in the works.

As mentioned earlier, Stratford's stud of J15s included a number of tripcock-fitted engines. These were sometimes used

One month before its withdrawal in September 1962, but nevertheless looking remarkably clean, No.65476 is still at work, caught during a pause in its shunting at Tottenham on 21 August. Note the weatherboard on the tender (which has 'sausage-shaped' frame slots) and the electrification flashes. The trip-cock gear can be seen alongside the leading guard iron. PHOTOGRAPH: PETER GROOM

Another version of the tender cab was fitted to No.65462, the engine which now survives on the North Norfolk Railway. It is seen here on the Stratford 'dump' on 27 September 1962, a week after withdrawal. This engine had been allocated to Lowestoft or Norwich for many years, and had latterly carried an imitation GER stovepipe chimney which had been constructed by Bill Harvey, the Norwich shedmaster, by welding on a new rim after cutting off the top of the usual Darlington-type chimney. No.65462 was finally transferred to Stratford in January 1961, and given trip-cock gear on arrival – this reflected the continuing need for engines to run over the LT Central Line. PHOTOGRAPH: PETER GROOM

on summertime excursion trains from LT stations; for example:
• During the summer of 1950 No.65453 was noted on Chingford-Southend (Victoria) trains
• On 19 July 1953 Nos.65450 and 65476 worked a Loughton-Eastbourne train as far as Liverpool Street
• On 4 July 1954 No.65476 took a Loughton-Brighton train, formed of seven

corridors, as far as Liverpool Street
• On 22 July 1954 Nos.65450 and 65476 (a familiar pairing!) took over a Dover-Chigwell special, formed of nine Southern corridor coaches, at Channelsea Curve, Stratford, and took them on to their final destination
• On 20 August 1955 No.65476 (clearly a favourite for this work!) was noted bringing an evening excursion into Southend.

Not all of this excursion traffic originated from Central Line stations. In August 1950, for example, No.65445 headed an Enfield-Southend (Victoria) train – it started out as one 'Quint-Art', but was probably joined by a five-coach half-set from another suburban station at Lea Bridge.

Enlightened readers (excuse the phraseology!) will be aware that, in the 1950s,

The other J15 to be 'Great Easternised' by Bill Harvey remained at Norwich until September 1961, when it was transferred to Cambridge. This was No.65469, seen here in May 1962, complete with its stovepipe, pottering about with a small steam crane. This is a particularly good view of the front-end fittings of a dual-fitted member of the class. PHOTOGRAPH: J.A.C.KIRKE; THE TRANSPORT TREASURY

No.65440 was built as GER No.640 in July 1899, the very first of the class to be dual-fitted. In this view, dated 16 February 1957, it is seen at Stratford, sporting one of the very short chimneys which were fitted to some of the class during the Second World War. This particular engine retained its chimney for the rest of its days. PHOTOGRAPH: R.C.RILEY

the illuminations at Southend generated considerable evening excursion traffic, and were just as big an attraction to Eastenders as the Blackpool Illuminations were 'Oop North'. The J15s were used on the Southend Illumination excursions – note the reference above to No.65476 on a Southend special in 1955. But as well

as holiday and excursion traffic, Stratford's J15s also made occasional appearances on ordinary scheduled passenger services. For example, on 29 April 1949, No.65476 was observed arriving at Gidea Park at the head of a suburban set, and in February the following year No.65455 was noted standing at Stratford (Low

Level) with a 'Quint-Art' for North Woolwich.

The Hertford (East) line was a particularly favoured route for the J15s. The little engine shed at Hertford (East) actually had two or three J15s allocated there until the early 1950s, but these were for goods duties, not passenger work. Those

Another of the first order of mixed traffic Y14s was GER No.645 which, as No.65445 of Colchester, is seen at the head of a two coach Witham-Maldon (East) train on 10 May 1958, passing a splendid ex-GER fixed distant. The 0-6-0s took over passenger duties on this branch for a few months in the Spring of 1958, filling in between the withdrawal of the last of the F5 2-4-2Ts and the arrival of the German diesel railbuses. PHOTOGRAPH: R.C.RILEY

This picture is a bit of a poser. The engine is No.65445, the location is alongside Brunswick Junction Signal Box at Poplar, and the date is 9 March 1964. The engine had been withdrawn from Stratford shed in August 1962, yet here it is, apparently in good shape, more than eighteen months later. It is in company with Departmental No.33, the Stratford Works Y4 0-4-0T which had not been taken out of service until December 1963, and what looks a B1 4-6-0 (or at least its tender). As far as we can determine, what happened is this – when Stratford ceased scrapping steam locomotives at the end of 1963 some of those which still remained, including No.65445 and Departmental No33, were sold to commercial breakers in the East End. This would appear to be the line up for cutting up by Messrs. A.King & Son. PHOTOGRAPH: PETER GROOM

which appeared on passenger work at Hertford (East) were usually Stratford engines. Among the reports of J15s on passenger duties on the Hertford (East) line is that of No.65440 which worked commuter trains to Liverpool Street for three consecutive days in February 1953. Early the following September, No.65464 was observed on several occasions on the 6.05am from Stratford. This latter engine had the CIE's 'flying snail' emblem on one side of its tender after having been used during the filming of *O'Leary Night* on the Buntingford branch! Apparently, the film featured David Niven and Yvonne de Carlo and was retitled *Happy Ever After* prior to release in this country. A few years later, on 27 December 1958, No.65440 was noted arriving tender-first at Liverpool Street with a passenger train from Hertford. Even as late as December 1961, J15s were being sent down to Liverpool Street as pilots because of a shortage of 800hp diesels.

Two or three trip-cock fitted J15s were sub-shedded at Epping for the goods and other steam-hauled workings over the electrified Central Line and out to Ongar. Although diesels took over the Epping line freight services in January 1959, J15s still occasionally appeared – for example, No.65476 was noted shunting at Woodford in the last week of December 1960.

For many years, fitted Stratford engines had been provided as pilots at Chelmsford and Romford, shunting the goods yards but available to assist or take over from any casualty. By the 1940s the Romford pilot job was regularly filled by a J39 but, at Chelmsford, J15s were still employed and, on 2 September 1948, No.65448 was observed working the up *East Anglian* from Chelmsford to Liverpool Street, complete with headboard.

By 1953 only two steam-brake J15s remained at Stratford, but there was still plenty of work for them. This included trip working between Temple Mills and Goodmayes Yards, pick up goods to Angel Road, Tottenham, the Lea Valley line and the Churchbury Loop, or to Abbey Mills and the North Woolwich branches. Many of these turns, and those such as the daily goods to Wood Street (Walthamstow), and to the Romford 'Factory' at Gidea Park (the old Eastern Counties workshops, part of it latterly used as the local goods yard) were shared with ex-works engines of other classes. And, as already noted, the Stratford 'snowplough' job was also a J15 duty.

COLCHESTER (30E): Until losing its allocation to Stratford, after nominally closing to steam in November 1959, Colchester shed was notable in that it kept ten or more J15s year after year. Like

Cambridge, with which it shared many duties, most of Colchester's J15s were vacuum-fitted engines. These worked the Colchester-Cambridge services via both Sudbury and the Colne Valley & Halstead lines. In addition, Colchester's pair of tender cab engines, Nos.65424 and 65432, were very often used on the Brightlingsea branch.

Colchester provided a J15 for pilot duties at Marks Tey, and another which combined shunting duties at Kelvedon with goods duties on the Tollesbury branch. Colchester's J15s also worked goods traffic from Witham to Maldon and, less frequently, to Braintree. Between the withdrawal of the last F5 and F6 2-4-2Ts from Colchester early in 1958 and the entry into traffic of the German diesel railbuses in July of that year, the J15s were often used on the passenger services on the Maldon and Braintree branches. For example, No.65470 was observed on the Braintree service on 10 May 1958 and No.65456 on the Maldon line two weeks later.

Colchester's J15s also appeared on goods, and occasionally on passenger workings, on the Clacton and Walton branches. On 28 June 1958, D16/3 No.62511 arrived at Colchester with an eight-coach train from Birmingham, which it had worked from Ely; its replacement for the final lap of the journey was J15

DISTRIBUTION OF J14 and J15 0-6-0s UNDER LNER AND BR
NF denotes steam brake only; F denotes Westinghouse and/or vacuum-fitted

	1.1923			1.1947		5.1950		1.1953		1.1959		1.1961		Remarks
	J14	NF	F	NF	F	NF	F	NF	F	NF	F	NF	F	
STRATFORD (30A)	5	74	17	23	10	5	14	2	13	1	7	1	6	
COLCHESTER (30E)	5	12	2	4	10	4	9	0	11	0	9	-	-	Closed 11.59; locos to Stratford
PARKESTON (30F)	1	2	0	2	1	2	1	1	2	1	2	-	-	
CAMBRIDGE (31A)	0	41	7	12	11	4	10	1	11	0	6	0	3	
MARCH (31B)	1	17	0	4	0	2	0	1	1	1	1	1	1	
KING'S LYNN (31C)	2	5	0	8	0	3	0	1	0	0	0	-		Closed 1.59; locos to Cambridge
BURY ST.EDMUNDS (31E)	0	0	0	1	1	2	1	1	0	-	-	-	-	
NORWICH (32A)	1	31	5	14	5	6	7	2	4	0	2	0	2	
IPSWICH (32B)	1	25	7	9	4	8	4	3	3	2	4	0	0	
LOWESTOFT (32C)	0	7	0	5	2	6	1	3	2	0	2	0	0	No J15s after 11.1947
YARMOUTH (32D)	1	3	1	1	2	0	0	0	0	0	0	-	-	Allocation briefly in 1947/48 only
YARMOUTH BEACH (32F)	-	-	-	0	0	0	0	0	0	0	0	-	-	Allocation briefly in 1947 only
MELTON CONSTABLE (32G)	-	-	-	0	1	0	0	0	0	0	0	-	-	From 7.1953
HITCHIN (34D)	0	0	0	0	0	0	0	0	0	0	1	0	0	2 x fitted locos 7.1957 to late 1958
NEASDEN * (34E)	0	0	0	0	0	0	0	0	0	0	0	0	0	None after late 1920s
LINCOLN (40A)	0	3	0	0	0	0	0	0	0	0	0	0	0	1 x non-fitted loco 5.61 to 11.61
NEW ENGLAND (35A/34E)	0	0	0	0	0	0	0	0	0	0	0	0	0	Closed 5.1939
PETERBOROUGH EAST	1	12	1	-	-	-	-	-	-	-	-	-	-	
TOTALS	18	232	40	83	47	42	47	15	47	5	34	2	12	
GRAND TOTAL	272 + 18			130		89		62		39		14		

* Neasden locos sub-shedded at Aylesbury

No.65451 (actually a Cambridge engine). Another example of the continuing use of J15s on passenger work in the Tendring Hundred was witnessed on 22 August 1958 when No.65467 arrived at Thorpe-le-Soken, tender-first, at the head of three corridors forming the Walton-on-the-Naze portion of a Clacton-Liverpool Street service. Once again the J15 was not a Colchester, but a Stratford, engine,

PARKESTON (30F): Steam-brake J15 No.65434, and fitted Nos.65453 and 65458 were allocated to Parkeston throughout the 1950s. They were used mainly on local freight workings between Harwich, Parkeston Quay and Manningtree. They also worked the short branch down to the mills and quay, on the banks of the Stour at Mistley.

Parkeston's fitted J15s occasionally appeared on passenger trains. There is a well-known photograph of No.65452 – with a medium length chimney and a storm sheet – on a Colchester-Harwich passenger train near Manningtree; it is undated but was clearly taken in mid-winter with leafless trees and a sharp frost on the sides of the cuttings. No.65452, which was probably a replacement for the more usual N2 0-6-2T on the Colchester-Harwich job, was not a Parkeston or Colchester engine, but was from Stratford – as will be apparent, 'common-usership' was a fairly regular practice in the Stratford District.

CAMBRIDGE (31A): The situation at Cambridge was similar to that at Colchester in that there was a substantial

contingent of J15s here throughout the 1950s, many for passenger work.

The Cambridge J15s' regular jobs included passenger work to Colchester – these turns were shared with Colchester J15s, but the Cambridge engines often worked through to Clacton or Walton during the summer. They also worked the goods traffic on the Audley End-Saffron Walden-Bartlow line, and were used on the Mildenhall branch (working alongside E4 2-4-0s).

At the end of 1950 Cambridge took over responsibility for the Huntingdon-Kettering line from the London Midland Region, and the J15s (which, since 1948, had monopolised the St.Ives-Huntingdon section) subsequently worked through from St.Ives to Kettering. The engine of the early morning train to Kettering

Bairds & Scottish Steel No.1, hard at work at Gartsherrie Ironworks at Coatbridge on 15 March 1956. This 'Little Goods' was the most-travelled member of the class, and a remarkable survivor. It was one of the forty-three which served with the ROD in France from February 1917 to June 1919, and was the last of the true Worsdell engines in service when withdrawn by the LNER in June 1938. It was then sold, becoming the only 'industrial' J15, and spent the rest of its working life at Coatbridge until retirement in 1958. As LNER No.7690 it had been fitted with a steel-roofed cab and Darlington-style chimney in the 1930s, but by the time this photograph was taken it had acquired a locally-made stovepipe and a brass dome cover. Clearly, this engine was kept in excellent cosmetic condition by its Scottish owners. PHOTOGRAPH: W.A.C.SMITH

spent the day pottering about on carriage shunting duties there before its return home in the evening. Although Ivatt Class 2 2-6-0s and, later, their BR Standard equivalents, subsequently took over most of the St.Ives-Kettering workings, J15s continued to appear on the line until 1957.

Two or three of Cambridge's J15s were usually sub-shedded at Ely for use on station pilot duties and also on goods duties on the St.Ives branch (which had lost its passenger services in 1931). Another Cambridge J15 was sub-shedded at Huntingdon. Following the down-grading of Bury St.Edmunds to the status of a sub-shed of Cambridge, another J15 was outstationed there and another at Sudbury. (Bury St.Edmunds closed in January 1959; Sudbury also seems to have been closed at that time).

By the end of 1961 only two J15s remained at Cambridge – these were Nos.65457 and 65469, the latter having recently been transferred from Norwich. A visitor to Cambridge on 12 November 1961 reported that both were on shed, out of use. No.65457 was withdrawn in February 1962, and No.65469 followed suit six months later.

MARCH (31B): In their early days, and even after the introduction of larger GER freight locomotives such as the G48 and F58 (later LNER J16 and J17) class 0-6-0s, many Y14s/J15s were allocated to March – no less than fifty-seven were shared with Peterborough (East) in 1907. However, in LNER days O4 and, later, O2 2-8-0s were sent to March and this brought about a cascade – the 2-8-0s took over duties which had hitherto been the domain of J17, J19 and J20 0-6-0s, and

so these 0-6-0s were downgraded and displaced most of the J15s. Nevertheless, there were still duties on some lighter lines in the Fens for which only the J15s were suitable. They were used in conjunction with J17s on the Three Horseshoes-Benwick branch, and also worked pick-up freights to Whittlesea and took water to isolated signal boxes and crossing keepers' cottages 'out in the sticks'. From May 1952 they took over on the Wisbech Harbour goods line, hitherto a King's Lynn job; this duty was normally given to a fitted J15, presumably because of the amount of van traffic.

By 1950 the March complement of J15s had fallen to just two steam-braked examples, but the shed retained two of the class until very late in the day; the last, No.65420, went south to Stratford in June 1962.

The manner in which this March presence was maintained is of interest, and is worthy of record as it is representative of what went on at other sheds where a 'Route Availability 1' engine was essential:

• At the beginning of 1950 March had two steam-braked J15s, Nos.65366 and (6)5349.

• No.(6)5439 was withdrawn in November 1951 (by which time it was the oldest steam-braked J15); it was replaced in December 1951 by No.65356, formerly of Cambridge (this was one of the two vacuum-fitted engines without a side-window cab, and was therefore less useful for the many passenger turns there).

• No.65366 was withdrawn June 1952; it was replaced in August 1952 by steam-braked No.65422 from Ipswich.

• No.65422 was withdrawn July 1955; by

this time there were very few steam-braked J15s left, and so its replacement, No.65474, formerly of Cambridge, was a dual-fitted example.

• No.65356 was withdrawn April 1957; there was no immediate replacement, and so No.65474 was left on its own until the end of 1958.

• Steam-braked No.65420 was transferred from Bury St.Edmunds in December 1958. (Bury St.Edmunds shed was about to close).

• No.65474 was withdrawn in February 1960 and replaced the following month by dual-fitted No.65458, which had become available as a result of the closure of its home depot, Parkeston. By this time, several small diesel shunters had been allocated to March and so the position of the J15s became somewhat anomalous; nevertheless, the two J15s (Nos.65420 and 65458) remained at work, and were no doubt more reliable than some of the early diesels.

• No.65420 was transferred to New England (q.v.) in May 1961, but it returned to March in November 1961

• No.65420 was transferred to Stratford (still in service) in June 1962. It was theoretically replaced by dual-fitted No.65469, which had been languishing out of use at Cambridge. However, the transfer did not actually take place. No.65469 *did* leave Cambridge (on 18 June) but, instead of going to March, it went to Stratford for scrapping.

• No.65458 remained at March until being withdrawn in October 1961.

KING'S LYNN (31C): At the start of 1947 King's Lynn had eight steam-brake J15s on its books. However, by May 1952

Pictured during its activities around Ipswich station on 10 August 1953, No.65404 is seen in close-up and displays the uncluttered buffer beam of a steam-braked engine. PHOTOGRAPH: J.ROBERTSON; THE TRANSPORT TREASURY

Allocation of J15s from January 1947 onwards

N.B: The following numbers are either the BR numbers (where applied) or the '1946' LNER numbers.

(VF) denotes vacuum-fitted; (T) denotes trip-cock fitted.

* Nos.5393 and 65466 were used as stationary boilers at Ilford Carriage Sidings and Melton Constable respectively after withdrawal

5350: at 1.47 – Cambridge; **wdn. 2.51**
5351: at 1.47 – Lowestoft; **wdn.5.49**
5352: at 1.47 – Norwich; 7.47 – Lowestoft; **wdn.5.48**
5353: at 1.47 – Lowestoft; 4.49 – Norwich; 5.49 – Ipswich; **wdn.12.49**
5354: at 1.47 – Stratford; 1.50 – Parkeston; **wdn.2.51**
5355: at 1.47 – Lowestoft; **wdn.4.51**
65356 (VF): at 1.47 – Cambridge; 12.51 – March; **wdn.4.57**
5357: at 1.47 – Colchester; **wdn.9.49**
5358: at 1.47 – Norwich; **wdn.8.47**
65359: at 1.47 – King's Lynn; **wdn.12.55**
5360: at 1.47 – Norwich; **wdn.11.47**
65361: at 1.47 – Stratford; 10.51 – Colchester; 11.50 – Ipswich; 1.57 – Stratford; **wdn.9.62**
5362: at 1.47 – Bury St.Edmunds; **wdn.7.51**
5363: at 1.47 – Stratford; **wdn.8.49**
5364: at 1.47 – Cambridge; **wdn.6.49**
5365: at 1.47 – Parkeston; **wdn.7.50**
65366: at 1.47 – Cambridge; 5.49 – March; **wdn. 6.52**
5367: at 1.47 – Norwich; **wdn.1.50**
5368: at 1.47 – King's Lynn; **wdn.5.48**
5369: at 1.47 – Cambridge; 7.49 – Stratford; 11.49 – Colchester; **wdn.2.51**
65370: at 1.47 – Stratford; **wdn.4.56**
5371: at 1.47 – Cambridge; **wdn.12.49**
65372: at 1.47 – March; 5.49 – Cambridge; **wdn.9.49**
5373: at 1.47 – Norwich; **wdn.10.50**
5374: at 1.47 – Stratford; 6.47 – Colchester; 5.48 – Lowestoft; **wdn.11.50**
5375: at 1.47 – Stratford; **wdn.11.49**
5376: at 1.47 – Stratford; 8.47 – Parkeston; **wdn.6.49**
5377: at 1.47 – Ipswich; **wdn.2.51**
65378: at 1.47 – King's Lynn; **wdn.4.51**
5379: at 1.47 – Cambridge; **wdn.9.49**
5380: at 1.47 – Stratford; 6.47 – Cambridge; **wdn.1.48**
5381: at 1.47 – Stratford; **wdn.11.48**
5382: at 1.47 – King's Lynn; 1.50 – Ipswich; **wdn.3.52**
5383: at 1.47 – Cambridge; **wdn.2.48**
65384: at 1.47 – Colchester; 1.50 – Stratford; **wdn.3.55**
5385: at 1.47 – Colchester; 6.48 – Stratford; **wdn.12.48**
5386: at 1.47 – Ipswich; **wdn.1.50**
5387: at 1.47 – Stratford; **wdn.8.49**
65388: at 1.47 – Stratford; 11.50 – Norwich; 3.52 – Ipswich; 9.52 – Norwich; 1.58 – Ipswich; **wdn.5.59**
65389: at 1.47 – Norwich; 8.47 – Lowestoft; 12.56 – Ipswich; 3.60 – Parkeston; **wdn.4.60**
65390 (VF): at 1.47 – Yarmouth; 6.47 – Norwich; 5.51- Cambridge; 6.52 – March; 8.52 – Cambridge; 7.57 – Neasden; **wdn.12.58**
65391 (VF): at 1.47 – Cambridge; 8.52 – Bury St.Edmunds; 10.52 – Cambridge; 11.53 – Bury St.Edmunds; **wdn.12.58**
5392: at 1.47 – Stratford; 2.49 – March; **wdn.5.49**
5393: at 1.47 – Stratford; 11.48 – Cambridge; **wdn.8.49** *
5394: at 1.47 – Norwich; **wdn.5.48**
5395: at 1.47 – Stratford; 2.49 – March; **wdn.5.49**
5396: at 1.47 – King's Lynn; 1.50 – Ipswich; **wdn.3.51**
5397: at 1.47 – Stratford; **wdn.9.49**
65398: at 1.47 – Norwich; **wdn.2.52**
5399: at 1.47 – Cambridge; **wdn.3.48**
5400: at 1.47 – Lowestoft; **wdn.2.48**
5401: at 1.47 – Norwich; 7.48 – Lowestoft; **wdn.9.51**
5402: at 1.47 – Stratford; 2.48 – Colchester; **wdn.10.50**
5403: at 1.47 – Norwich; **wdn.8.47**
65404: at 1.47 – Stratford; 6.47 – Norwich; 11.51 – Ipswich; **wdn.10.56**
65405 (VF): at 1.47 – Cambridge; 8.52 – Bury St.Edmunds; 10.52 – Cambridge; 11.53 – Bury St.Edmunds; ? – Cambridge; 7.57 – Neasden; **wdn.8.58**
5406: at 1.47 – Cambridge; **wdn.4.51**
5407: at 1.47 – Ipswich; **wdn.4.51**
65408: at 1.47 – Norwich; 9.49 – Ipswich; **wdn.12.51**
5409: at 1.47 – Ipswich; **wdn.11.49**
5410: at 1.47 – Stratford; 6.47 – Cambridge; **wdn.2.48**
5411: at 1.47 – Norwich; **wdn.4.48**
5412: at 1.47 – Cambridge; 11.48 – Stratford; **wdn.10.49**
5413: at 1.47 – Cambridge; **wdn.11.50**
5414: at 1.47 – Colchester; **wdn.11.49**
5415: at 1.47 – Ipswich; **wdn.5.49**
5416: at 1.47 – King's Lynn; **wdn.12.49**
65417: at 1.47 – Norwich; 3.47 – Melton Constable; 6.47 – Norwich; 2.48 – Melton Constable; 4.48 – Norwich; **wdn.8.56**
5418: at 1.47 – Stratford; **wdn.3.48**
5419: at 1.47 – March; 2.48 – Norwich; **wdn.2.50**
65420: at 1.47 – Cambridge; 7.47 – Bury St.Edmunds; 12.58 – March; 5.61 – New England; 11.61 – March; 6.62 – Stratford; **wdn.8.62**
5421: at 1.47 – Ipswich; **wdn.3.48**
65422: at 1.47 – Norwich; 4.51 – Ipswich; 8.52 – March; **wdn.7.55**
5423: at 1.47 – Ipswich; **wdn.11.50**
65424 (VF): at 1.47 – Colchester; 12.59 – Stratford; **wdn.12.59**
65425: at 1.47 – King's Lynn; 10.49 – Cambridge; **wdn.10.56**
65426: at 1.47 – Yarmouth; 2.47 – Norwich; **wdn.5.51**
5427: at 1.47 – Stratford; 1.50 – Colchester; **wdn.10.50**
5428: at 1.47 – Stratford; 6.47 – Ipswich; **wdn.8.49**
5429: at 1.47 – Ipswich; **wdn.11.50**
5430: at 1.47 – Ipswich; **wdn.1.56**

the shed had only one of the class, No.65359, which remained there until being sent to Stratford for withdrawal in December 1955. Much later, on 26 May 1959, No.65451, a Cambridge locomotive, was noted working as the King's Lynn station pilot. It is very probable that representatives of the class continued to make sporadic visits to King's Lynn after this date.

BURY ST. EDMUNDS (31E):

At the Grouping in 1923 this shed was part of the Ipswich District and did not have its own permanent allocation. However, in June 1938 it was transferred to the Cambridge District and became an independent shed, rather than a sub-shed. During World War II Bury St.Edmunds acquired several J15s for use on traffic for the many airfields and military facilities in that part of East Anglia; some of the engines were fitted with spark arresters for working the sidings of the ammunition depot at Barnham on the Bury-Thetford branch. After the withdrawal of No. (6)5362 in mid-1951, only No.65420 remained, but this engine soldiered on until Bury St.Edmunds shed closed in January 1959. During the 1950s, No.65420 – sporting its spark arrester on a succession of chimneys of different types – worked the Thetford branch goods. On one occasion in August 1952, F6 2-4-2T No.67222 failed at Barnham while working the three-

coach Bury-Thetford service and No.65420 came to the rescue; the J15 propelled the outfit to its destination and then piloted the ailing tank engine back to Bury St.Edmunds on the return working.

Bury St.Edmunds also had a solitary fitted J15, No.65442, which undertook some passenger work. On 13 September 1951 it even worked the Bury St.Edmunds portion of *The Fenman* forward from Cambridge instead of the usual 'Claud' – for this duty, the humble J15 proudly carried the train headboard!

When No.65442 was transferred away to Cambridge in August 1952, Bury St.Edmunds received in return all three of Cambridge's fitted tender-cab J15s. They stayed only briefly, but the following year two of them, Nos.65391 and 65405, returned. By this time the passenger service to Thetford had ceased, but as these two Bury St.Edmunds J15s had tender-cabs, they came in very useful for the sub-shed at Sudbury which, because it lacked a turntable, had plenty of tender-first running along the rural branches.

NORWICH (32A):

At the end of World War II Norwich had had more goods (i.e. steam brake) J15s than any shed apart from Stratford. They were used on the numerous light goods and pick-up freight services which meandered across Norfolk. Norwich also had around half-a-dozen fitted J15s for use on passenger workings on various Norfolk branch lines; they often shared these duties with the delightful little E4 2-4-0s. Among the passenger workings were the County School-Wroxham and Thetford-Swaffham services, and also the Dereham-North Elmham milk trains. Some of Norwich's J15s were outstationed at sub-sheds; Dereham, for example, still had four in 1950. At the height of the holiday season, Norwich's J15s were liable to be pressed into service on station pilot work or shunting empty stock at the Norwich (Thorpe) terminus; they were also used to haul passenger trains from the Midlands and elsewhere on the last leg of their journey to the Norfolk coastal resorts.

Norwich's J15s also worked passenger services on the Waveney Valley line (Tivetshall-Beccles), until the services ceased in January 1953 (see also under Lowestoft). Despite the cessation of the ordinary passenger services, summer excursions continued to originate on the Waveney Valley line – usually to the seaside at Yarmouth – for a few more years. These excursions had become a regular feature of the line and, going back to *circa* 1948/49, the first post-war outing was formed of two 'Quint-Arts' which had been made redundant from the Liverpool Street suburban services. By the early 1950s, though, eight corridors were the norm, and this necessitated double-heading – on one particular occasion in September 1952, J15 No.65471 and E4 No.62789 were observed working in unison.

Inevitably, Norwich's stud of J15s fell steadily as the years progressed. From nineteen in 1947, it was reduced to just six in 1953 and, by the late 1950s, it was

65431: at 1.47 – Parkeston; 8.47 – Stratford; 9.49 – Colchester; **wdn.3.51**

65432 (VF): at 1.47 – Colchester; **wdn.3.58**

65433: at 1.47 – March; 2.49 – Norwich; 6.49 – Lowestoft; 3.55 – Ipswich; **wdn.1.58**

65434: at 1.47 – Stratford; 7.49 – Parkeston; 1.50 – Stratford; 8.50 – Parkeston; **wdn.11.59**

65435: at 1.47 – Lowestoft; 1.48 – Norwich; 2.48 – Lowestoft; 8.55 – Ipswich; **wdn.10.56**

5436: at 1.47 – Stratford; 2.48 – Colchester; 6.48 – Stratford; **wdn.12.49**

5437: at 1.47 – King's Lynn; **wdn.9.50**

65438 (VF): at 1.47 – Cambridge; 8.52 – Bury St.Edmunds; 10.52 – Cambridge; **wdn.6.58**

5439: at 1.47 – March; **wdn.11.51**

The remaining engines were all dual-fitted in LNER/BR days:

65440 (T): at 1.47 – Colchester; 2.48 – Stratford; 10.50 – Colchester; 11.50 – Stratford; 4.51 – Colchester; 7.51 – Stratford; **wdn.10.60**

65441 (T): at 1.47 – Stratford; 6.50 – Colchester; **wdn.10.58**

65442: at 1.47 – Bury St.Edmunds; 8.52 – Cambridge; **wdn.5.58**

65443 (T): at 1.47 – Colchester; 10.52 – Stratford; 9.58 – Colchester; **wdn.12.59**

65444 (T): at 1.47 – Stratford; 5.50 – Colchester; 9.50 – Stratford; **wdn.10.58**

65445: at 1.47 – Colchester; 11.59 – Parkeston; 1.61 – Stratford; **wdn.8.62**

65446 (T): at 1.47 – Stratford; 11.49 – Colchester; 9.50 – Stratford; 3.51 – Parkeston; 7.51 – Stratford; 1.59 – Colchester; 12.59 – Stratford; **wdn.12.60**

65447: at 1.47 – Ipswich; **wdn.4.59**

65448: at 1.47 – Cambridge; 6.47 – Colchester; 12.59 – Stratford; **wdn.3.60**

65449 (T): at 1.47 – Stratford; **wdn.12.59**

65450 (T): at 1.47 – Stratford; 11.58 – Cambridge; **wdn.10.61**

65451: at 1.47 – Cambridge; **wdn.9.59**

65452 (T): at 1.47 – Stratford; **wdn.12.59**

65453 (T): at 1.47 – Stratford; 6.47 – Parkeston; 2.48 – Stratford; 7.51 – Parkeston; 1.61 Stratford (stationary boiler at Ipswich by late '61); **wdn.8.62**

65454 (T): at 1.47 – Colchester; 6.47 – Stratford; 6.50 – Colchester; 9.50 – Stratford; 11.58 – Ipswich; **wdn.5.59**

65455 (T): at 1.47 – Stratford; **wdn.3.60**

65456: at 1.47 – Colchester; 9.49 – Stratford; 10.49 – Colchester; **wdn.9.58**

65457: at 1.47 – Cambridge; **wdn.2.62**

65458: at 1.47 – Stratford; 8.47 – Parkeston; 3.60 – March; **wdn.10.61**

65459: at 1.47 – Ipswich; 12.59 – Stratford; **wdn.2.60**

65460: at 1.47 – Norwich; 9.55 – Lowestoft; 9.60 – Norwich; 12.60 – Stratford; **wdn.9.62**

65461: at 1.47 – Cambridge; **wdn.4.60**

65462 (T): at 1.47 – Lowestoft; 3.47 – Norwich; 11.47 – Lowestoft; 7.60 – Norwich; 1.61 – Stratford; **wdn.9.62**

65463 (T): at 1.47 – Colchester; 6.47 – Stratford; **wdn.11.59**

65464 (T): at 1.47 – Stratford; **wdn.9.62**

65465: at 1.47 – Ipswich; 6.47 – Colchester; 12.59 – Stratford; **wdn.9.62**

65466 (T): at 1.47 – Colchester; 6.47 – Stratford; 7.53 – Colchester; **wdn.7.58 ***

65467: at 1.47 – Ipswich; 1.57 – Stratford; **wdn.2.59**

65468: at 1.47 – Cambridge; 6.47 – Stratford; 6.50 – Colchester; **wdn.9.59**

65469: at 1.47 – Yarmouth; 3.47 – Norwich; 9.47 – Yarmouth; 11.47 – Yarmouth Beach; 2.48 – Norwich; 7.57 – Lowestoft; 9.57 – Norwich; 9.61 – Cambridge; (6.62 – March*); **wdn.8.62** (*transfer to March not effected; loco went from Cambridge to Stratford for withdrawal)*

65470: at 1.47 – Norwich; 6.48 – Ipswich; 7.48 – Norwich; 4.49 – Ipswich; 11.50 – Colchester; **wdn.12.59**

65471: at 1.47 – Lowestoft; 2.47 – Norwich; 10.49 – Lowestoft; 11.49 – Norwich; **wdn.6.60**

65472: at 1.47 – Melton Constable; 3.47 – Norwich; 1.48 – Yarmouth Beach; 2.48 – Norwich; 8.57 – Yarmouth; 9.57 – Norwich; 8.58 – Colchester; 12.59 – Stratford; **wdn.12.59**

65473: at 1.47 – Norwich; 6.47 – Colchester; 12.59 – Stratford; **wdn.3.60**

65474: at 1.47 – Cambridge; 5.55 – March; **wdn.2.60**

65475 (T): at 1.47 – Colchester; 6.47 – Stratford; 7.49 – Cambridge; 9.49 – Colchester; 10.49 – Cambridge; **wdn.9.59**

65476 (T): at 1.47 – Parkeston; 6.47 – Stratford; 3.50 – Colchester; 7.51 – Stratford; **wdn.9.62**

65477: at 1.47 – Cambridge; **wdn.2.60**

65478: at 1.47 – Norwich; 3.49 – Lowestoft; 4.49 – Norwich; 7.50 – Lowestoft; 3.59 – Ipswich; 3.60 – Cambridge; **wdn.10.61**

65479: at 1.47 – Norwich; 11.48 – Lowestoft; 2.49 – Norwich; 11.50 – Colchester; 7.53 – Hitchin; **wdn.8.60**

---

down to just two. The last two were Nos.65469 and 65471. In 1960, the Norwich shed-master, Bill Harvey, gave the pair special cosmetic treatment, removing the rims from their chimneys to create very credible imitations of Holden stovepipes. No.65471 was almost immediately withdrawn, but was replaced by No.65462, from Lowestoft, which then ran with No.65471's chimney. Nos.65462 and 65469 both appeared on a number of enthusiasts' specials, but No.65462 did not stay long, moving on to Stratford in January 1961. No.65469 remained at Norwich until September of that year, when it too

left for Cambridge. Its departure marked the end of the J15s' lengthy association with Norwich shed.

IPSWICH (32B): In the summer of 1947 J15s took over the working of the Mid-Suffolk Light Railway from the small J65 0-6-0Ts; this had been made possible by the relaying of the line with bull-head rails. A dual-fitted J15 was outstationed at Laxfield for the passenger and mixed trains on the Mid-Suffolk line, and a second steam brake engine was provided for goods traffic. No.65447 was a particularly regular performer on the 'Middy' (*see RAILWAY BYLINES 5:4, March 2000*) and had the distinction of working the final passenger service between Haughley and Laxfield on 26 July 1952. Thereafter No.65388 and subsequently No.65404 were employed clearing this rural byway and hauling the demolition trains. The dual-fitted Ipswich J15s appeared from time to time on the Aldeburgh branch passenger services, and No.65447 headed the last steam working on 9 June 1956. The J15s were also used on end-of-term school specials on the Framlingham branch – No.65459 officiated in March 1954 and again in May 1955.

In 1954 a weekday goods left Ipswich at 9.00am for Framlingham and returned at 11.55am; this job was often combined with a trip to Snape Maltings. The latter branch was finally closed in March 1960 – Nos.65389 and 65478 had worked the branch in its final months. The J15s also had local turns around Ipswich, including trip working to the docks and to Felixstowe. More than a dozen of the steam-brake J15s ended their days at Ipswich in the 1950s, replacements

being drafted in from other sheds as withdrawals took place. One of the class, often on its last legs, was usually employed as the shed pilot.

LOWESTOFT (32C): Lowestoft retained an allocation of J15s until 1960. They worked the eastern end of the Waveney Valley line between Bungay and Beccles (this section was restricted to RA2 locomotives), and undertook a number of local goods turns to Oulton Broad (South), Kirkley and Lowestoft Harbour South. The Harbour job included the working of piped or braked fish vans to the junction with the East Suffolk line. Lowestoft lost its last three steam-brake engines, No.65389, 65433 and 65435, to Ipswich in 1955/56, but retained three dual-fitted J15s, Nos.65460, 65462 and 65478, for another four years.

Even during the 1950s, the Lowestoft J15s occasionally took over the Lowestoft portion of *The Easterling* and other London-Yarmouth services for the last lap from Beccles and, like their counterparts at Norwich, were kept busy during the holiday season. In 1953, No.65478 was recorded at the head of eleven corridors *en route* from Yarmouth (Beach) to Lowestoft via the Norfolk & Suffolk Joint (formerly M&GN and GER Joint).

YARMOUTH SOUTH TOWN (32D) and YARMOUTH VAUXHALL (32E): At the beginning of 1947 there were three J15s allocated to 'Yarmouth' (the LNER seems not to have given separate listings for each of the two ex-GER sheds), but all were soon transferred to Norwich; the only engine of the class to return was No.65472 which was sent from Norwich to Vauxhall for a few weeks in the summer of 1957.

MELTON CONSTABLE (32G) and YARMOUTH BEACH (32F): These two sheds had once been part of the Midland & Great Northern Railway and had been taken over by the LNER as recently as 1936. Consequently, they were not traditional J15 strongholds. Indeed, the only allocation of J15s to either shed was in 1947/48 when Nos.5417 and 5472 spent brief periods at Melton Constable, and Nos.5469 and 5472 were briefly at Yarmouth Beach.

Given this scenario it was somewhat ironic that, after No.65466 was withdrawn in July 1958, it went to Melton Constable for use as a stationary boiler and remained there until after the closure of the M&GN in 1959. Furthermore, the preserved No.564 (BR No.65462) has found a permanent home on the old M&GN at Weybourne, the headquarters of the North Norfolk Railway.

PETERBOROUGH (EAST) and NEW ENGLAND (35A/34E): Prior to its closure in May 1939, the ex-GER shed at Peterborough (East) had housed numerous J15s. The class was also represented at the town's ex-Great Northern shed at New England in the 1930s, but it was not until May 1961 that any of the class reappeared there. The incomer in 1961 was No.65420 (by this time one of the last

Vacuum-fitted J15 No.65405 was photographed from the single lengthy main line platform face at Cambridge on 10 August 1954. It was one of the class to have a short chimney. PHOTOGRAPH: J.ROBERTSON; THE TRANSPORT TREASURY

two surviving steam-brake J15s), but the engine was required only for working the engineer's train which was undertaking the demolition of the St.Ives-Huntingdon (East) line and, when that task was completed later that year, it returned to March.

..........ooooo000ooooo..........

In their early years the Y14s had worked from the Great Eastern sheds at Doncaster and Lincoln, but after the Grouping they were rarely seen outside East Anglia. A few were briefly shedded at Doncaster, Barnsley and Mexborough during World War II, and some were scrapped at Doncaster (for example, Nos.7842, 7868, 7870 and 7938 in January 1935), and at Darlington (No.5380 in January 1948 among others) but, otherwise, their wanderings were few and far between. That said, in March 1947 No.5372 was observed shunting at York – this was, admittedly, a somewhat extreme example!

Despite the class's general tenacity to familiar territory during the LNER period, in the 1950s there were two notable transfers to 'foreign parts':

HITCHIN (34D): In July 1953 a Colchester J15, No.65479 – the 'baby' of the class – was transferred to Hitchin. It remained there until August 1960 when it was dispatched to Doncaster for scrap. J15s had not been unknown in the Hitchin area in LNER days, working in from Cambridge from time to time, but the principal pur-

No.65461 hauls a single ex-LMS brake van, no doubt on the way to work a local pick-up goods. A Cambridge engine by 1947, it was still there when withdrawn in 1960, but at various times was recorded sub-shedded at Ely, Sudbury and Bury St.Edmunds. It was also reported at Kettering, Mildenhall and Chappell, an indication of the range of duties undertaken by Cambridge J15s. PHOTOGRAPH: W.HERMISTON; THE TRANSPORT TREASURY

One of the last two steam-braked engines to survive was No.65420. By June 1960 – when it was photographed at the head of a very long string of wagons at March – it was one of the small allocation at March. The depot's huge coaling plant is in the background, and on the left is the stern warning: *ENGINEMEN MUST BRING THEIR ENGINES TO A STAND AND PROCEED IF THE LINE IS CLEAR.* PHOTOGRAPH: J.A.C.KIRKE; THE TRANSPORT TREASURY

pose behind No.65479's transfer there in 1953 was for the weekend leave trains to and from RAF Henlow, on the Midland branch to Bedford. This job had previously been worked by J1 0-6-0 No.65013. The J15 led a very quiet life itself as, apart from the weekend trains to and from Henlow, it ventured out only occasionally, usually to work a pick up goods along the Hitchin-Hertford (North) line.

NEASDEN (34E/14D): In June 1957 two vacuum-fitted J15s, Nos.65390 and 65405 (the latter having a tender cab), were transferred to Neasden from Cambridge and Bury St.Edmunds respectively. That said, one of the two locomotives was actually outstationed for a week at a time at Aylesbury (the other being kept as a spare) to work goods traffic on the former GWR Princes Risborough-Watlington branch following the cessation of the branch passenger services. Most of the freight was associated with the cement works at Chinnor. However, the J15s lasted barely a year on these duties; No.65405 was withdrawn in August 1958 and No.65390 followed four months later. Scrapped at Stratford they were, incidentally, the last two engines of the class which had served with the ROD in France.

Undertaking a typical J15 passenger job, No.65457 of Cambridge shed waits for departure in the branch line platform at Marks Tey on a sunny afternoon in May 1958. PHOTOGRAPH: J.A.C.KIRKE; THE TRANSPORT TREASURY

Stationary boiler service

Three J15s are known to have been used as stationary boilers, though there were undoubtedly others as well.

• No.5393 – withdrawn from Cambridge in August 1949; used at the then new Ilford Carriage Sidings from August 1950 until January 1951.

• No.65466 – withdrawn from Colchester in July 1958; observed at Melton Constable in May 1959 (this was after the closure of Melton Constable shed and the cessation of M&GN passenger services).

• No.65453, still nominally in traffic and allocated to Stratford, was in use as a stationary boiler at Ipswich in October 1951 where it supplied steam to the wagon repair shop for about a month before being returned to Stratford.

Author's acknowledgements: Thanks are due to Mr.Lyn Brooks of the GER Society for invaluable advice and assistance. For details of membership of the GER Society, send an s.a.e. to Mr.J.R.Tant, 9 Clare Road, Leytonstone, London E11 1JU. (The society's quarterly journal is worth the membership fee alone – Ed.).

Right. The 5.10pm Cambridge to Colchester train is ready to leave Bartlow, the junction for the Saffron Walden branch, on 25 August 1956. It is headed by No.65468 – one of Colchester's numerous allocation – which is gently blowing off. The starter is yet another fine ex-GER signal. PHOTOGRAPH: R.C.RILEY

Below. The amount of freight generated by the branch lines of East Anglia, even in the mid-1950s, was still very respectable. Here, No.65467 of Ipswich passes Woodbridge with the pick up for the Framlingham and Snape branches on 10 October 1956; the train comprises 30 or more assorted wagons and vans. PHOTOGRAPH: R.C.RILEY

Cambridge's No.65451 at work as the Kings Lynn station pilot on 26 May 1959. By this date, the withdrawal of the mixed traffic J15s was well under way, and this particular example had less than three months left before its final one-way trip to Stratford. PHOTOGRAPH: J.A.C.KIRKE; THE TRANSPORT TREASURY

A NEW BRIDGE AT PINNER

Photographs by C.R.L.Coles

On Sunday 30 May 1954, the bridge which carried the joint London Transport/Eastern Region line over Chapel Lane, just to the north of Pinner station, was renewed. These fascinating pictures provide a brief glimpse of the day's work. In the upper picture on this page we see the engineer's train; the locomotive, Westinghouse- and tripcock-fitted L49, is one of the former Metropolitan Railway's 'F' class 0-6-2Ts, while the brake van on the left-hand line is B552, which had started life with the Metropolitan in 1890. The pictures right and below show the bridge work in progress. The crane appears to be the 50-ton Cowan Sheldon & Co machine which had been purchased by the Metropolitan in 1925 (but we stand to be corrected!).

While the work was in progress the train services between Northwood and Pinner were necessarily suspended, passengers being conveyed between those two

stations by bus. This indirectly provided a bit of treat for local railway enthusiasts – as the Metropolitan Line trains from Aylesbury had to terminate at Northwood, and as the schedules did not allow adequate time for the locomotives to run round there, the trains had a locomotive fore and aft for the 3½ miles between Rickmansworth and Northwood.

Among the pairings noted were L1 2-6-4Ts Nos.67440 and 67447, and 67792 and 67800. It was remarked that this section of the old Met line had rarely seen so many steam-hauled trains since 1925 when 'the juice' had been extended to Rickmansworth.

ISLE of MAN TRAMS – a miscellany

Photographs by W.J.Ford (all taken Whitsun 1959). Notes and captions by Tom Heavyside

Snaefell Mountain Railway car No.6 has passed the photographer and is about to round the north shoulder of the mountain, shortly after beginning the long descent from the summit station back to Laxey. Contrary to normal practice in the British Isles, right-hand running is the norm on Snaefell. The railway climbs 1,820 feet during the 4¾-mile run from the starting point at Laxey, the ruling gradient being 1 in 12. During their sojourn at the top, passengers will have had the opportunity to visit the refreshment rooms and clamber the extra 46 feet to the summit of Snaefell itself, from where, on a clear day, it is possible to see parts of England, Scotland, Ireland and Wales. The raised 'third rail' on the right-hand track is the Fell rail which is used for braking purposes and also to provide some extra stability on this exposed section of the route; it will be noticed that there is no Fell rail in the centre of the left-hand (ascending) track. The back-cloth to this superb picture is provided by the 1,808 foot peak of Clagh Ouyr.

Arguably, the Isle of Man is best known for the annual TT (Tourist Trophy) motorcycle races. These take place over a very testing 37¾-mile course along public roads, and every year thousands of people flock across the Irish Sea to witness the riders circuiting the island at average speeds in excess of 120 miles per hour. For those whose preferences are geared to somewhat more sedate forms of transport, some of the main attractions of the island are undoubtedly the exquisite vintage narrow gauge railway and tramway systems.

In the RAILWAY BYLINES SUMMER SPECIAL No.1 we featured the steam-operated Isle of Man Railway. Here, we take a brief look at the other main systems on the island, namely the Manx Electric Railway and the Snaefell Mountain Railway, both of which owe their existence to the island's late nineteenth century growth in popularity as a tourist destination.

The longer of the two tramways is the 17¾-mile overhead electric railway which links Derby Castle, at the north end of Douglas Promenade, with Ramsey, the principal town in the north of the island. The first 2½-mile section from Derby Castle to Groudle was opened in 1893 under the auspices of the Douglas & Laxey Coast Electric Tramway Co. The following year the track was extended from

Groudle through to Laxey, the railhead at first being situated on the south side of Glen Roy, near to the present car sheds. In that same year, 1894, the company purchased the Douglas Horse Tramway, and the corporate title was changed to the Isle of Man Tramways & Electric Power Co Ltd (IoMT&EP), a title which was also in keeping with its aim of generating electricity for sale to other customers as well as for its own use. Two years later, in 1896, the IoMT&EP decided to extend the route further north to Ramsey. This was completed in 1899.

At the time, electric traction was a comparatively new innovation, but was considered to be the best option in view of the sinuous, very steeply-graded switchback route that was necessary in order to negotiate the very difficult terrain along

the east side of the island. The overhead wires carried current at 500 volts.

As already indicated, visitors to the island have always been the main source of income for the island's railways but, importantly, the new electric railway also provided a much needed lifeline for some of the small isolated communities dotted along its route. For many years goods were also carried, including cattle and sheep, along with stone from the quarries at Dhoon. A contract to carry the mail was ended as recently as 1975.

Turning our attention to the Snaefell Mountain Railway, this was promoted by a private syndicate which mainly comprised directors of the IoMT&EP. The SMR opened for business in August 1895, but at the end of the year the railway was sold to the IoMT&EP, the proprietors re-

The southern terminus of the Manx Electric Railway is at Derby Castle, at the north end of Douglas Promenade. Here, car No.19 has already had its trolley pole changed round to the end nearest the camera in preparation for its next journey north to Ramsey. No.19 is in a livery of red, white and teak. It was the first of four winter saloons built by G.F.Milnes of Birkenhead in 1899; each car had 48 seats. The winter saloons were originally fitted with four 20hp engines and Milnes bogies. However, in 1904 the Manx Electric Railway took delivery of four cross-bench open cars (Nos.28 to 31) from the Electric Railway & Tramway Carriage Company of Preston; these had slightly more powerful 25hp engines and improved Brill bogies. When these new cars were delivered, it was decided that these new engines and bogies would be better employed under the winter saloons and they were exchanged accordingly. No.19 was fitted with the engines and bogies from No.29. The horse trams terminate behind the booking office on the left. Sadly, the fine canopy that provided shelter at the end of the horses' journeys along the promenade from the Sea Terminal was removed as an economy measure in 1980, much to the chagrin of many people. Note the hoarding on the left which makes much of the Rover ticket – two days unlimited travel on the MER for ten bob.

Car No.21 has just left Groudle station on its way south towards Douglas. This car is another of the winter saloons constructed by Milnes in 1899. It is painted in the green and white livery which had been adopted by the railway following Nationalisation in 1957, though this was later abandoned in favour of the traditional red, white and teak. Other points of interest are the large headlight and the clerestory roof. On the left can be seen the Groudle Hotel, and just to its right is the archway over the entrance to the glen, a much-frequented beauty spot. From the gateway a steep path leads down into the glen and also gives access to the 2ft gauge Groudle Glen Railway, one of the very few railways that runs uphill to the sea! Regrettably, at the time of the photographer's visit in 1959, the Groudle Glen Railway was closed. It was operational in 1961 and 1962, but it was subsequently dismantled. However, it has since been restored, and one of the mainstays of the service is the line's first steam locomotive, the diminutive 2-4-0T SEA LION, which had been built by Bagnall's in 1896 as their Works No.1484. The Groudle Glen Railway runs regularly on Sundays during the summer and also operates on certain evenings in high season; in connection with this, the Manx Electric Railway operates a shuttle service from Derby Castle, using a specially illuminated car.

Manx Electric Railway car No.5, with an unidentified trailer in tow, pauses at Groudle, opposite the hotel and the entrance to the glen, on its way back to Douglas. Groudle was the northern terminus of the line when the first section of single track tramway was opened in 1893 (the line was doubled in 1894), and a plaque to mark the centenary was unveiled here on 7 September 1993. No.5 is one of six vestibuled saloons, numbered 4 to 9, which were supplied by Milnes in 1894. They were built to carry 36 passengers on longitudinal seats, but in 1932 No.5's seating arrangements were revised to a '2+1' formation along with four in each bulkhead, which reduced its capacity to 32. Four of these cars are still available for use, including No.5. Regrettably, cars Nos.4 and 8 were among the rolling stock which was destroyed by a disastrous fire at Laxey Car Sheds in 1930.

Shortly after leaving Groudle, going north, the line swings sharply through 180° in order to cross the glen by means of a lofty three-span viaduct, the parapet of which can just be seen on the right. Here we see car No.19 again, this time passing the old toll house *en route* to Ramsey; the roadway, incidentally, had been built at the same time as the tramway. At the rear is trailer No.44, a 44-seat cross-bench open built by English Electric in 1930. It is, in fact, a replacement trailer car for the original No.44 which had been supplied by Milnes in 1903 – this was another casualty of the 1930 Laxey fire. The trailers, most of which are open, are very popular on hot sunny days, but on this occasion it appears that many of the travellers preferred the close confines of the saloon, rather than brave the breezes which sweep directly off the Irish Sea along some sections of the route.

alising a very good return from their initial investments.

The Snaefell line started at Laxey. When the line first opened, passengers boarded the cars by the SMR car sheds but, in 1897, the line was extended down the hill as far as the main road. A further short stretch of track was opened in 1898, after which the cars used the present interchange station with the Douglas-Ramsey route.

From Laxey the line rises almost to the summit of Snaefell, the highest peak on the island at 2,036 feet above sea level. The gauge chosen was 3ft 6in, and while the cars are more than capable of clambering the steep slopes by adhesion alone, a Fell rail was laid down the centre for braking purposes and to help prevent derailments by adding some extra stability. A voltage of 550 was passed through the overhead wires.

Although the fortunes of the island's tramways were initially good, in February 1900 matters turned rather sour for the directors and shareholders of the IoMT&EP when the island was thrown headlong into a serious financial crisis, due to the sudden collapse of Dumbell's Bank. Many businesses and scores of private individuals were hit by the bank's closure, not least the IoMT&EP which was

forced into liquidation. Fortunately, the Isle of Man Railway was left almost unscathed by the debacle, for either through luck or good management, the majority of its assets were lodged elsewhere.

There were many long hours spent in various negotiations regarding the disposal of the assets of the IoMT&EP before Douglas Corporation came to the rescue of the horse tramway in 1901. Then in 1902 an agreement was reached with a consortium based in Manchester for the sale of the Ramsey and Snaefell lines, only for them to be sold within a few weeks, for a somewhat handsome profit, to the newly-established Manx Electric Railway. The MER was to operate the two railways, except for wartime interruptions on the mountain line, for over 50 years.

During the 1950s, with the numbers of visitors to the island in serious decline, the MER found it increasingly difficult to maintain the services, and in 1955 the company decided that it had little alternative other than to close down completely at the end of 1956, and it duly advised the Manx Government to this effect. Thankfully, Tynwald, the Manx Parliament, stepped in and purchased the business in 1957.

Although the MER came under the control of the Manx government, questions

have occasionally been asked regarding the future of the MER, particularly in respect of the route north of Laxey. Indeed, the MER was closed in its entirety for the winter in October 1975 and, the following summer, services along the route north of Laxey remained suspended. After much lobbying and debating within Tynwald regarding the future of the island's railways, the Ramsey line was reopened in June 1977.

Despite the various problems that have beset the island's railways over the years, it is pleasing to report that the two systems under review here remain intact and are in regular use during the summer months; there is also a limited service on the Manx Electric Railway in the winter period. Over the years, many improvements have been made to the rolling stock and the infrastructure, including the electrical supply and associated equipment, but the tramways have managed to remain very much as they were in the late Victorian era, each exuding its own particular charm. Be assured, a warm welcome awaits any who care to travel across the Irish Sea to examine them in a little more detail. *(Thanks to Douglas Robinson for assistance in the compilation of these notes and captions).*

Laxey is the main town served by the Manx Electric Railway between Douglas and Ramsey, and in high season a number of extra services are run to Laxey from Derby Castle. Arriving from Ramsey is car No.20, another of the 1899-built winter saloons; it is painted in the post-1957 green and white livery. The conductor/guard looks out from the rear platform, no doubt eyeing up a group of potential passengers, some perhaps anxious to return to Douglas in time for high tea. A distinctive feature of this location are the palm trees (on the right); behind is the Mines Tavern, another popular island watering-hole – it was actually owned by the railway prior to 1957. Beyond is the goods shed which dates from 1903.

Laxey is the interchange station between the Manx Electric Railway and the 3ft 6in gauge Snaefell Mountain Railway. Six cars were manufactured by Milnes for the opening of the latter in 1895, each powered by four 25hp engines and with seating for 46 passengers. Within a couple of years the seating capacity had been increased to 48 by installing an extra seat against each bulkhead, and about the same time clerestories with windows were fitted as an aid to ventilation. Car No.3, with No.6 just visible on the right, awaits its next trip up the mountain. The cars are in a similar red, white and teak livery to their Manx Electric counterparts, although two were painted green and white for a time after the Manx Government became responsible for the line in 1957. The 'Big Wheel', referred to prominently by the board on top of the car is the gigantic 72½-foot diameter Laxey Wheel, also known as 'Lady Isabella'. This is one of the island's most noted landmarks – it was erected in 1854 to pump water from the lead mines and, although eventually falling into disuse, it was purchased by the Government in 1965 and is now fully restored. In the foreground of this picture is a short section of mixed gauge track, which was used when the Snaefell cars needed to be transferred to Douglas for heavy maintenance. Prior to the move to the Derby Castle workshops they had to be jacked-up and the wheel-sets run from underneath before being slewed sideways three inches, in order to centre the cars over the 3ft gauge track. They were then placed on accommodation bogies being ready for the journey south. Improvements to the SMR car sheds at Laxey in the early 1990s have made it possible to undertake all the maintenance requirements at their own depot, thereby obviating the need to transport the cars to Derby Castle.

At a height of over 1,300 feet above sea level, car No.6 eases across the main A18 Douglas to Ramsey 'mountain' road at the Bungalow (originally known as Halfway) before halting for a short time during its ascent towards the summit of Snaefell. This is the only intermediate station on the line. The Fell rail, which is positioned four inches above the outside rails, is for obvious reasons absent on the crossing. The car's two bow-shaped current collectors are clearly visible. The A18 road forms part of the TT course, the railway crossing being just short of the 31 mile marker, and on race days the riders hurtle past this point at speeds in excess of 100mph. The TT races obviously interrupt some of the tramway operations at this particular location – tramway passengers travelling to Snaefell have to cross the road by means of a footbridge to a second car which is waiting on the summit side of the crossing. Almost inevitably, though, many passengers take a prolonged break to enjoy the racing! At one time the passengers could enjoy a drink in the railway-owned hotel at The Bungalow; the hotel was constructed in 1896, but was demolished in 1958. As can be well imagined by those not familiar with the area, there are some spectacular scenes to be enjoyed from the comfort of the electric cars, first from the right hand side as the magnificent Laxey Wheel gradually recedes into the distance. From the Bungalow onwards the emphasis changes to the other side of the car as the beauty of Sulby Glen and the reservoir appear way down below, and then, as the car grinds its way further round the mountain, the town of Ramsey and Point of Ayre, the northern tip of the island, come into view – that is provided the upper slopes are not shrouded in mist!

SCREEN TEST

Denby Hall Colliery was situated close to the ex-Midland Railway branch between Ambergate and Ripley. The branch was closed to ordinary passenger traffic in 1930 but was retained for goods traffic, principally coal from the collieries along its route. In the early 1950s a surface drift was opened up at Denby Hall and new plant was installed. This set of pictures shows the new surface set-up, presumably some time in the early or mid-1950s. This first picture gives a good view of the loaded wagon sidings. The four loaded wagons in the centre of the picture are descending to the weighbridge (out of view behind the photographer); the wagons' descent is being controlled by the two men – these were 'wagon lowerers' – who applied the brakes when necessary.

A mixed rake of wagons – five-plank and six-plank wooden, older steel-bodied and modern 16-ton – pass to the loaded sidings. The small coal in these wagons would have been loaded from a hopper as breakage is not important for small coal. The conical tower is part of the washery.

Cobbles are being loaded into a seven-plank wagon by means of a 'boom loader' conveyor which is lowered into the wagon in order to minimise breakage. As the wagon is filled, the conveyor is raised.

Another view of the boom loader in action. The ex-LMSR 'high goods' wagons were often used for house coal in the 1950s. The wagon on the extreme left is a colliery 'internal user'.

A rake of 16-ton mineral wagons – including a couple which appear to be virtually new – pass from the empties sidings on their way to be loaded. As for Denby Hall Colliery, it merged with the nearby Denby Colliery in January 1967, but the new arrangements lasted only until February 1968 when production ceased. However, the branch line remained open to serve a disposal point for coal from open cast workings which were a little to the east of Denby Hall. But that, too, has now come to an end, the disposal point having closed early in 1999. *(Thanks are due to Mr.Roy Etherington for assistance with the preparation of these notes).*

FOURUM – narrow gauge in Kent
Photographs by W.J.Ford

Messrs.Bowater's Lloyd's paper mill at Sittingbourne in Kent was famed among railway enthusiasts for its extensive 2ft 6in gauge system. The system was very intensively used until the mid-1960s. Four of the locomotives were distinctive-looking Kerr Stuart 0-4-2STs. The last of the four to be delivered was MELIOR (W/No.4219 of 1924) – it was similar in most respects to the other three, but had Hackworth valve gear instead of Stephenson's. This picture was taken at Ridham Dock, possibly in September 1956.

The very first locomotive to be delivered to Bowater's was Kerr Stuart 'Brazil' class 0-4-2ST PREMIER (W/No.886) which was despatched by the makers in August 1905. Given that the locomotives would be working in and around stacks of paper, they were fitted from new with spark arresters. The first type of spark arresting equipment took the form of wire grids inside the smokebox, but this was later superseded by 'balloon stack' arresters, as seen here. However, the 'balloon stacks' were found to hinder the locomotives' steaming capabilities and so the 'wire grid' equipment was reinstated. Nevertheless, several of the locomotives retained their balloon stacks despite the fact that they no longer served a purpose. Another point of interest here is the locomotive's dumb buffer.

CONQUEROR was a W.G.Bagnall 0-6-2T (W/No.2192), purchased new in 1922. Until the early 1950s it was the heaviest locomotive on the Bowater's system and was prohibited from traversing the viaduct at the Sittingbourne Mill end of the line. In later years it was used almost exclusively at Ridham Dock. Note the new style of centre buffer and semi-automatic coupling; these started to be fitted to the Bowaters locomotives from the mid-1950s.

W.G.Bagnall 0-6-2T SUPERB (W/No.2624) was the last of three similar locomotives purchased new between 1932 and 1940; this fine portrait shows it with its original dumb buffer. The principal functions of Bowater's narrow gauge railway were to transport woodpulp from the dock and quays to the mill and finished paper back to the dock for loading on board ships, but it also had an internal passenger service for members of staff. To give an idea of the scale of operations on this railway system, in the late 1950s and early 1960s, it dealt with 180,000 tons of woodpulp, 150,000 tons of paper and an estimated 75,000 passengers annually. Nevertheless, the narrow gauge system was taken out of use in 1968, but no less than thirteen of the sixteen locomotives were saved for preservation. The four shown here have all been saved; fittingly, MELIOR, PREMIER and SUPERB are now on the Sittingbourne & Kemsley Light Railway which occupies part of the former Bowater's system. *(A major article about Bowater's narrow gauge railway appeared in the July 1998 edition of RAILWAY BYLINES – that's Vol.3 No.5 – Ed.)*

The Irish Transport Company, C.I.E. (Coras Iompair Eireann), was formed in 1945 to administer all forms of public land transport wholly in Eire, as the twenty-six counties were then known. The largest constituent of CIE was the Great Southern Railways whose creation in 1925 had been by order of the newly-formed Free State government. The 'grouping' of 1925 had brought together under the Great Southern banner several standard gauge railway companies (the Irish standard gauge was 5ft 3in); these included the Great Southern & Western (the largest railway company in Ireland), the Midland Great Western, the Dublin & South Eastern, the Cork Bandon & South Coast, the Cork & Macroom Direct, the Timoleague & Courtmacsherry and the Waterford & Tramore. Here, we shall take a random look at a few of the standard gauge branch lines which eventually passed from the Great Southern to CIE.

> **Abbreviations used:**
> **CB&SCR** – Cork, Bandon & South Coast Railway
> **CIE** – Coras Iompair Eirann
> **C&MDR** – Cork & Macroom Direct Railway
> **D&MR** – Dublin & Meath Railway
> **D&SER** – Dublin & South Eastern Railway
> **GNR** – Great Northern Railway
> **GSR** – Great Southern Railways
> **GS&WR** – Great Southern & Western Railway
> **MGWR** – Midland Great Western Railway
> **T&CLR** – Timoleague & Courtmacsherry Light Railway

If there were a typical Irish branch line, in a land singularly lacking in mineral resources, it was a line which was entirely rural and with a business wholly agricultural. For the benefit of English readers, the closest comparison would be with the country lines of the old Great Eastern Railway, which were also largely dependent on farming – including sugar beet production – and in LNER days were worked by obsolete locomotives, often 2-4-0s and small 0-6-0s. The branch passenger trains were often formed from a variety of elderly carriages, including six-wheelers – this heightened the similarity with the Irish branch line scene.

Many Irish branches began life as local enterprises that never raised enough capital and were in time swallowed up by a main line company – this, of course, has been heard before, as the authorisation and financing of Irish railways prior to 1921 was determined by the Westminster Parliament. It was the later period of Irish railway development that had to rely on Government subsidies of various kinds.

Other branch lines represented the rump of some grandiose trunk route never fulfilled. One such was the extension of the Dublin & Meath Railway which was intended to strike northwards from Navan to Armagh and develop as a rival route to the Great Northern Railway between Dublin and Belfast. However, the

BROAD GAUGE BRANCH LINES OI
An overview by Desmond Coakham

Dublin & Meath line stopped short at Kingscourt in County Meath, where the terminus had all the appearance of being intended as a through station. Happily, though, it is still with us; it is a rare example of an Irish mineral branch, being used for carrying gypsum from the local mines to Drogheda and beyond via the remnant of the GNR's Oldcastle branch.

Another example that springs to mind is the Mountmellick branch from Maryboro (Portlaoise) on the Cork main line. Here the branch train was propelled out of Maryboro on the Kilkenny line, to reverse at Conniberry Junction (¾ mile) and proceed northwards for 7½ miles to Mountmellick, passing under the Cork line *en route*. Mountmellick was once noted for its lace industry, but I don't imagine

that this generated too much rail traffic. The branch was intended to have been part of a northward extension of the Waterford & Central Ireland Railway from Kilkenny to Mullingar, from where it would have conveyed cattle to the port of Waterford.

In the 1930s, certain Dublin newspapers, worried about the loss-making GSR, used to call for what they termed 'railway surgery', in the assumption that the pruning of branches was the panacea for all railway ills. But by 1936 (the date of the GSR map that accompanies this article), few closures had taken place. The Kinsale branch (CB&SCR) and the narrow gauge around Cork city had gone, and the first couple of grant-aided extensions in Connaught – Galway to Clifden and Ballina

C.I.E.

The branch line from Limerick to the port of Foynes on the Shannon estuary has been an intermittent success story over the years. The branch has been in operation since 1858, beginning at Ballingrane on what used to be the North Kerry line of the Waterford & Limerick Railway from Limerick to Tralee. The latter was a pretty and under-rated route that never saw much tourist activity; one might say that Ireland has too much scenery in relation to the size of its tourist industry. The terminus at Foynes, 27 miles from Limerick, is shown as it was on 25 June 1959, exhibiting much of the layout and style of the 1850s. This view of the train shed from dead-end looks across the wagon turntable which led to various quay sidings. The locomotive is No 101, the much-rebuilt pioneer of the GS&WR '101' (or 'J15') class 0-6-0s which saw out steam on CIE. Today, the railway to Foynes is still in use in connection with the town's petrochemical industry. PHOTOGRAPH: DESMOND COAKHAM

to Killala — had also vanished from the map. The magnificent Achill line would go before World War II, but the remainder of the network was intact when the wartime fuel shortage caused havoc on the GSR and in the country as a whole. Coal imports from Britain virtually dried up, and this affected town gas supplies as well as railway services. The branches suffered worst of all, but they still survived; indeed, many branches had a brief revival after 1945, but that was brought to an end by the 1947 fuel crisis, which was largely due to an abnormally severe winter and its effect on railborne coal supplies in Britain.

From then on, many branch lines fell into torpor, barely kept alive by the necessity to serve the monthly cattle fairs and the seasonal football traffic. Under CIE administration, money was at last found for diesel propulsion and much needed rolling stock, to say nothing of paint for stations large and small. There was a welcome increase in passenger numbers, but the losses were never entirely eliminated. Experts were called in to report, and serious closures began in the 1960s, removing at consecutive strokes the scenic Kerry branches and the entire CB&SCR system. The demise of

The station at Sligo opened in July 1863 as the terminus of an 84-mile long secondary line from Mullingar on the Midland Great Western main line to Galway. There was, and still is, a mile-long harbour branch that deals with the town's goods traffic; in the 1950s and 60s this was enough to justify a resident shunting engine. The branch diverged just outside the Sligo terminus; the terminus also hosted the trains of the Sligo Leitrim & Northern Counties Railway whose line joined the MGWR at Ballysodare, six miles to the south. Our view of 29 May 1957 shows the station pilot, ex-MGWR 2-4-0 No.659, shunting the Sligo Mail into one of the two carriage sidings between the arrival and departure platforms – the station layout had shown little change in nearly a century. By 1957 the Mail was worked by Metrovick diesel locomotives (class A), the unpainted aluminium bodies of which quickly and horribly oxidised. The leading vehicle of the rake in our picture is a four-wheeled heating van, almost new, which provided steam heating for the train. Its matching livery is as yet unblemished. Next to it is the piece-de-resistance, a lovely old MGWR six-wheel TPO. It is in the earlier CIE two-tone green livery. The girder-work spanning between platforms in the background recalls the one-time all-over roof at the terminus. PHOTOGRAPH: F.W.SHUTTLEWORTH

those lines meant that their potential for the sophisticated rail tours like those now operated in the Scottish Highlands went untapped.

In general, the surviving branches remained steam-operated, though CIE made a token gesture of converting a road motor bus to rail operation in emulation of the successful GNR and County Donegal railbuses. But the corporate heart was not really in the project, and little was heard of the experiment.

Apart from its lengthy County Kerry branches, most offshoots of the GS&WR were relatively short connections to towns which had been by-passed by the trunk lines. A case in point was that from Goold's Cross to Cashel (5¼ miles), which opened in 1904 and closed to passengers in 1947. Cashel is on the main road from Dublin to Cork. So is the important town of Naas in County Kildare – this was 2¼ miles from Sallins on the Cork line and was the first station out on the Tullow branch. Only about 19 miles from the centre of Dublin and in today's terms part of the city's outer suburbia, Naas had lost its passenger services in that bleak year of 1947, along with the rest of the 34-mile branch. In the same general area but part of the Midland Great Western section, the old Dublin & Meath line from Clonsilla to Navan, 37 miles from Dublin by the inland route, was closed completely in 1963. There is now a strong possibility of

its partial reopening – providing that the E.U. milch cow does not run dry – as another outer suburban route for the expanding city.

But the old MGWR's archetypal branch lines were in 'cattle country' and had some delightful termini which were positively inspirational for the freelance modeller. Of these, we give you glimpses of Ballaghadereen and Loughrea. Other MGWR branch lines went to Ballinrobe and Killeshandra, Athboy (a twig off the Kingscourt branch) and Edenderry. The last-named town lay in the debatable territory south of the Midland main line and was the subject of much sabre-rattling between the MGWR and GS&WR in their formative years. The Southern company secured a foothold on the Shannon at Athlone, but the Midland denied it access to the main line station. Consequently, the GS&WR established its own terminus just short of the later (1860) junction. The GS&WR's Athlone branch left the Cork line at Portarlington and served large-ish towns at Tullamore and Clara en route. At the latter place it was joined by another 7¾-mile fragment of MGWR line, namely the Streamstown & Clara branch which had opened in 1863 and had been intended as a strategic thrust to stop the GS&WR advancing from Tullamore. It had never had any real value, but survived until 1965 with one intermediate station, Horseleap. I believe the name is

derived from the barbaric practice of disposing of old horses by driving them over a precipice.

However, the junction at Clara was a happier place for the enthusiast, having an exchange platform entirely separate from the main GS&WR station, with a compact but little used goods yard on the MGWR side; it also had a handsome signal cabin, more a 'signal tower', in fact, as it was a tall, brick building, four-square and dignified. Clara had another, wholly GS&WR, junction at the down end where the Banagher branch diverged to terminate on the banks of the River Shannon, 18 miles away across dreary bogland. The promoters of this line had a notion of crossing the Shannon to Meelick, in the wilds of Galway, but the line was completed only as far as Banagher, and that was by another company in 1884, no less than twenty-three years after first authorisation. The Banagher branch survived for goods only until 1962.

Off-hand, one can count no more than four railways crossing over Ireland's longest river, and one of these was the Arigna branch of the narrow-gauge Cavan & Leitrim Railway. By an irony of history the MGWR main line between Mullingar and Athlone is now virtually disused, the GS&WR Athlone branch having been upgraded to carry all traffic for Galway and the far west. Looking briefly at other constituents of the GSR, the Dublin & South

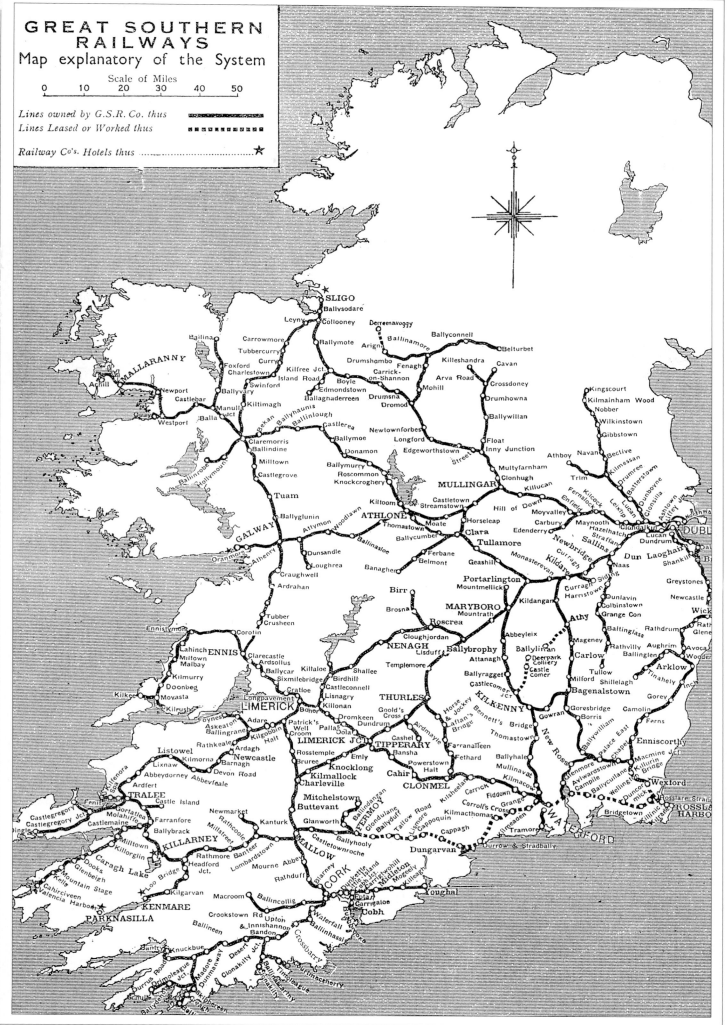

GREAT SOUTHERN RAILWAYS
Map explanatory of the System

Scale of Miles
0   10   20   30   40   50

Lines owned by G.S.R. Co. thus ▬▬▬▬▬
Lines Leased or Worked thus ▪▪▪▪▪▪▪▪▪

Railway Co's. Hotels thus .... ★

Sligo shed, 8 June 1957. A SLNCR locomotive had board and lodging at the MGWR, later GSR and CIE, engine shed at Sligo and, on the day of the author's visit, it was Beyer Peacock 0-6-4T ENNISKILLEN. She stands in front of the handsome Midland water tower and will later return eastwards on a cattle special. Note the engine coal store to the left of the locomotive. Visitors were shown this feature, massively walled in limestone and secured by large double iron doors, and told that it was to prevent the SLNCR enginemen from stealing the Midland coal! Shame on them for impugning a fine bunch of railwaymen. In fact, the 'security measure' was a standard MGWR feature. And you will notice that the doors are wide open! **PHOTOGRAPH: DESMOND COAKHAM**

Eastern Railway had only one genuine branch line; this was from Woodenbridge, in the Vale of Avoca, to Shillelagh (17 miles), the town that gives its name to the big stick (for thumping people), now made only for the souvenir market. The later line from Macmine Junction to Waterford would have been regarded by the D&SER as a main line, but the GSR had other thoughts.

Then there was the Cork & Macroom Direct Railway, which was 23½ miles in length from its headquarters in the Cork suburb of Capwell to Macroom. Sometimes described as the 'exclusive breth-

Ballaghadereen (who said Wales had all the tongue-twisters?) was the felicitous terminus of a 10-mile branch from Kilfree Junction on the Mullingar-Sligo line. Here are the characteristic Midland engine shed and water tower, built of the limestone which is plentiful in Ireland – the stone is easily worked, though rather porous. Another former MGWR 2-4-0, No.655 (with round-top firebox this time), is on shed. The turntable pit is in the foreground. Ballaghadereen had a long cattle bank but, in practice, its accommodation was effectively dictated by a very short shunting neck at the terminal buffer stops – this was not a typical MGWR layout, but was possibly a throw-back to the original promoters, the Sligo & Ballaghadereen Junction Railway. The branch had a life of 89 years, opening in February 1874 and closing in February 1963. **PHOTOGRAPH: W.A.C.SMITH**

Attymon Junction was 107 miles from Dublin (Broadstone) on the MGWR main line in County Galway. The nine-mile branch from the junction to Loughrea was a latecomer, being opened by the Loughrea & Attymon Light Railway in December 1890 and worked by the Midland Great Western. Attymon was a remote place among bogland; the railway was arguably its most important feature. There was a passing loop on the main line (it had been double-track from Dublin until a GSR economy drive which also closed Broadstone terminus – the latter was not too traumatic a loss as it was too far from the city centre). The Loughrea branch diverged from the down loop and running-round arrangements were elaborate, with a shunting neck alongside the main line at the up end, off which were an engine siding and turntable. The signal cabin, of the Midland style with internal staircase, lay in the fork between the main line and the branch, the latter having its own platform.

Flowerbeds intervened between the platforms, and the station building occupied the internal angle. Road access was from the north or down side of the main line by means of an overbridge, and a footbridge linked the up and down platforms. Local goods traffic was catered for by a shed on its own short siding which trailed into the up loop. All the buildings except the signal cabin were brick-built – this betrayed their comparatively recent origin. It seems fitting to have described this tidy little station in detail, as it was 'Midland' to the proverbial 'T'. This view shows the Loughrea mixed train on 7 June 1961, with ex-MGWR 0-6-0 No.610 in charge. The leading coach is the branch six-wheeler (brake third No.9M); it is followed by a modern four-wheeled parcels van and what may be an ex-MGWR bogie coach, with a respectable tail of goods vehicles. The station building is on the left. PHOTOGRAPH: W.A.C.SMITH

ren' of Irish railway companies, the C&MDR had been quite profitable in the 19th century. For many years it repelled the CB&SCR's attempts to forge a physical connection at Cork but, during World War I the government decreed that a connection must be made – this was to help to flow of traffic to and from an important military base on the line. After the war the connection was taken out of use and the C&MDR returned to a state of isolation. Following the grouping in 1925, the GSR lost no time in closing Capwell terminus and reinstating the junction with the old CB&SCR. Services were worked from the nearby Albert Quay terminus of the former CB&SCR. The Macroom line had an interesting stud of tank locomotives including an Andrew Barclay 0-6-2T of 1904; the company is even rumoured to have had a bogie carriage! Bus competition killed the Macroom line's passenger traffic, and the final closure to all traffic was brought about by flooding the Lee Valley for a reservoir in 1953.

I regret missing the fun of the seasonal excursion traffic on the last line to be mentioned – the Timoleague &

Courtmacsherry Light Railway. This was a sprig from the Clonakilty branch of the CB&SCR. It closed officially in the spring of 1961 but, when I visited in March of that year, it was moribund; I believe the last passenger trains had run during the previous summer. The T&CLR was, in fact, two companies worked as one: the Ballinascarthy & Timoleague opened in 1890 and the Timoleague & Courtmacsherry Extension in the following year. Both were Baronially guaranteed and lost money hand over fist, at the ratepayers' expense. Yet the nine miles from the junction to the pretty little seaside village known as Courtmac (for short) – with the last three miles in the form of a broad gauge roadside tramway twisting along the seashore – deserved a better fate. Freight traffic was almost non-existent at the end; during the season, the line was extremely popular and on Sundays was traversed by excursion trains through from Cork. For these trains the CB&SCR provided purpose-built short bogie carriages that could tackle the extreme curvature. They were, in GSR/CIE days, hauled by the petite

0-6-0Ts Nos.90 and 100 which wintered at Glanmire shed at Cork. The TCLR handed over two locomotives to the GSR in 1925; these were products of the Hunslet Engine Co – SAINT MOLAGA and ARGADEEN. Neither ever carried a number. SAINT MOLAGA, an 0-4-2T, went in 1949; ARGADEEN was, most unusually for the broad gauge, a 2-6-0T – she was small enough to be rebuilt with the boiler from a steam railcar. She finished her days shunting on the quays at Cork and was withdrawn in 1957.

As I have inferred, many of these by-ways perished before the majority of my own generation had an opportunity to visit them, and it has been left to a small nucleus of railway photographers, who could not have been everywhere at once, to leave us any record of past glories. In compiling this article, an invaluable work of reference has been Volume 16 ('Ireland') of the *Regional History of Railways* series (Atlantic Transport Publishers 1995) by J.W.P. Rowledge. *Johnson's Atlas & Gazetteer* (Midland Publishing, 1997) has also been consulted to advantage.

This photograph of 11 June 1957 shows another MGWR 2-4-0, No.654, on the branch train at Attymon Junction. On this occasion the bogie coach is GSR No.2101, a vestibuled lavatory composite of 1926; we also have a six-wheeler and a cattle wagon. The station nameboard is still the attractive MGWR pattern in enamelled sheet metal, with white letters on a dark blue background. It was made by a Birmingham company, and the style was widely adopted for railway notice boards.
PHOTOGRAPH: DESMOND COAKHAM

Another picture taken on 11 June 1957 – earlier that day, the up mixed train had been more substantial and is seen awaiting departure from Loughrea. It is viewed from the long cattle platform which occupied all the west side of the terminus. The brake third is out of view at the rear of the train. Loughrea station was symmetrical, and logically planned, with facilities which might be described as lavish. Did the MGWR lean heavily on the local company in view of its agreement to work the line? Or, since it was only a year after the Regulation Act of 1889, did the Board of Trade insist on up-to-date signalling and layout? The well-finished buildings were built of stone; the goods store was adjacent to station buildings and came complete with loading dock and crane. On the same side of the yard were the turntable, coal stage and engine shed (two roads, no less). There had also been a carriage shed, but that was the only item which had not escaped the economies of the 1930s. Loughrea, which had a population of 1,800 around the turn of the century, had to wait longer than most for its railway but, as if to confound the old adage of 'last in, first out', the Loughrea branch was actually the last of CIE's typical country branches to retain a passenger service. Closure did not come until November 1975. PHOTOGRAPH: DESMOND COAKHAM

This endearing specimen, CIE (ex-GS&WR) No.90, began life in 1875 as an 0-6-4T 'combined engine and carriage'. Designed under the auspices of Alexander McDonnell and built at Inchicore Works for the Castleisland Railway, it proved inadequate for the traffic – this, of course, was a familiar theme in the rail motor saga. Consequently, No.90's passenger accommodation was modified to conform with others of the type which toured the GS&WR system as 'pay cabs' – these were the vehicles which were used to take wages to the staff at outlying corners of the railway network. In the case of No.90, it was rebuilt to the form shown here in 1915, its light axle loading making it useful among the nooks and crannies of the GSR. No.90 and a similar engine, No.100, were retained until 1959. Shedded at Cork (Glanmire), their last duties included working the Timoleague & Courtmacsherry line, a roadside appendage of the West Cork system. No.90 was part of CIE's token gesture towards preservation, and was mounted on a pedestal at Mallow station on the Cork main line. It is seen here at Glanmire shed on 4 June 1961. PHOTOGRAPH: W.A.C.SMITH

The Cork Bandon & South Coast Railway, with a 62-mile main line from Cork (Albert Quay) to Baltimore, was not connected to the main network until the construction of the Cork City Railways in 1912. But this connection was made by means of a street tramway which incorporated two lifting bridges, and through passenger traffic was a rare occurrence. While there were branches serving picturesque seaside towns such as Kinsale, Clonakilty and Bantry, the pleasant area of West Cork was not really exploited until private motoring had gained an ascendancy. On the railway, dieselisation came too late to combat the road competition, and the entire network had closed by 1961. Here we see a typical Up mixed train leaving Skibbereen on the Baltimore line on 29 June 1950. The locomotive is a former GS&WR 2-4-2T, No.33, one of a variety of engines drafted on to the CB&SCR from other sections to replace worn-out native stock. One recalls an ex-Waterford & Limerick Robinson 4-4-2T, and other tank engines from the GS&WR and D&SER. Reverting to this picture, the photographer is standing with his back to the narrow gauge terminus of the Schull & Skibbereen Railway; this line had ceased operations during the fuel shortage of 1947, but everything was still in place three years later. (More about this in *Railway Bylines* eventually!). PHOTOGRAPH: IVO PETERS

An earlier portrait of a 'Kerry Bogie' on Kenmare turntable, embowered with foliage, on 24 October 1949. The climate on the south-west coast of Ireland is described as sub-tropical; palms and other exotics flourish, but those high mountains can attract the rain. The GSR adopted a form of locomotive classification very similar to that used on the LNER, and these 4-4-0s were 'D19'. But locomotive men usually referred to them by the old GS&WR method whereby the running number of the initial engine was the class designation – in this case, the 'No.2' class. PHOTOGRAPH: IVO PETERS

Left. The 1890s were boom years for Irish railway construction. The need to improve communications with the remoter and more disadvantaged parts of the island coincided with an upsurge in the British tourist industry and persuaded the Government to provide funds for railway building in the Far West. County Kerry, with the lakes of Killarney already accessible by rail, was particularly fortunate in being a natural goal for the joint undertaking of the GS&WR and Great Western Railway whose object was to forge a new east-west route from the port of Rosslare, joining and improving strategic pieces of existing railway. The old-established GS&WR line from Mallow to Killarney and Tralee was now linked directly with the channel ports. From the Tralee line, two important branches were made; both were opened in 1893. One of those branches went to Valentia Harbour and the other to Kenmare, the terminus of the latter being 22 miles from Headford Junction near Killarney. The Kenmare branch passed through wild country before meeting the Atlantic at the head of Kenmare Bay. One supposes Kenmare to be the anglicised form of 'Ceann Mara' – head of the sea – but the bilingual nameboard in this photograph appears to read 'NEIDIN' in Gaelic characters, proving that Celtic placenames are a great source of dispute. At Parknasilla, a few miles down the coast of Kenmare Bay, the GS&WR built one of several 'Great Southern' hotels in an attempt to stimulate the tourist traffic. Road excursions, by horse-drawn brakes and later motor charabancs, were a great feature of those early days. The famous 'Ring of Kerry' still attracts the private motorist, though the present writer freely admits never having ventured far from steel rails. In common with other stations on both branches, Kenmare had timber-framed buildings clad with corrugated iron; this simplicity had been essential, as most of the capital had been swallowed up by ferociously expensive civil engineering work. This picture of Kenmare station was taken in June 1951. One obvious feature of the layout is that the rails are of very light cross-section – they are probably original, and they tend to exaggerate the broad gauge to some extent. The mixed train awaiting departure is headed by 4-4-0 No.13, one of McDonnell's last class for the GS&WR (and the first 4-4-0s in Ireland), which were introduced in 1877. PHOTOGRAPH: IVO PETERS

Below. The other branch which opened in 1893 was that to Valentia Harbour. It was even longer than the Kenmare line, being no less than 40 miles from its junction, which was at Farranfore. The first 12 miles had been opened by a local company in 1885. Their terminus was at Killorglin, where the line ended in a substantial train shed. When the line was driven on towards the Atlantic coast, a second platform was added to what became the new up loop of the new block post. In this view from the footbridge, an Up mixed train enters Killorglin. Little has changed apart from the motive power, this being Metrovick diesel-electric No.C229 which contrasts with the solitary six-wheeled carriage. The GNR(I) van visible on the Down train (in the foreground) had been acquired by CIE at the previous year's 'divvy-out' between it and the Ulster Transport Authority. The date is 26 June 1959. Both these branches were to succumb in 1960, leaving the scenery as sole prerogative of the motor vehicle. PHOTOGRAPH: DESMOND COAKHAM

HEREFORD TO BRECON –

The 38½-mile line between Hereford and Brecon opened throughout in September 1864. The section between Hereford and Three Cocks Junction belonged to the Hereford, Hay & Brecon Railway, the rest of the journey into Brecon being by means of running powers over other companies' lines. The Hereford, Hay & Brecon was eventually leased by the Midland Railway, whereas the lines over which it had running powers eventually became part of the GWR. The route therefore acquired two distinct identities – east of Three Cocks Junction it was Midland, later LMSR, while west of the junction it was GWR.

The separatism prevailed until 2 April 1950 when, under the glasnost of the British Railways era, the Western Region was given control of the whole line. The WR put 'Dean Goods' and occasionally 2251 class 0-6-0s to work on the line, but some of the turns were still entrusted to ex-Lancashire & Yorkshire 0-6-0s which were based at Hereford shed. The L&Y engines were very unpopular with the Hereford crews, partly on account of their scanty cabs (but it must be said that, for this very same reason, the 'Dean Goods' were also less than popular). In 1952 the WR looked at alternatives to the 'Dean Goods' and the Lanky 0-6-0s – this was not so much out of concern for the crews, but be-

cause the two types of 0-6-0s were somewhat ancient and would need replacing before too long anyway. In the spring and early summer of 1952, trials were conducted with 57XX class 0-6-0PTs and, although these were considered to be successful, there was soon a major change of heart. In June of that year, four ex-Midland Class 3 0-6-0s were transferred to Hereford principally to take over the passenger turns on the Brecon line.

With the ex-Midland engines on the passenger turns and with ex-GWR 'Dean Goods' and 2251s on the freight jobs, it was not immediately evident to the unwary visitor that the Hereford-Brecon line was part of the Western Region. Indeed, the old HH&B section of the line (Hereford to Three Cocks Junction) retained its traditional Midland/LMS-style fixtures and fittings, right down to the station nameboards. In fact, the 'foreign' aspect was considerably emphasised in 1953 when the working of the line was given over to LMSR-designed locomotives – the Ivatt Class 2 2-6-0s. Five of these – Nos.46518, 46521, 46522, 46523 and 46524 – were allocated to Brecon (89B), partly for use on the Hereford line.

By this time, doubts had already been expressed about the line's future. At one stage there had been rumours that the passenger services were to be withdrawn;

The date is Monday 6 June 1960 and the location is Eardisley, 14¼ miles along the line from Hereford. The driver of No.46506 has time for a brief chat while exchanging the staff before proceeding to Hereford with the 10.25am from Brecon. The station building on the left-hand platform might look a little familiar to some readers – after its removal from Eardisley it was acquired by the Welshpool & Llanfair Railway and re-erected at Welshpool. PHOTOGRAPH: HUGH BALLANTYNE

he final years

subsequent rumours hinted at the cessation of through trains between Hereford and Brecon, with services terminating at Three Cocks where they would connect with Mid-Wales trains to and from Brecon. But the rumours proved to be false, and things remained largely unchanged throughout the remainder of the 1950s.

The following decade was, however, a very different matter. In 1961 the BTC proposed the closure of the Hereford-Brecon line. In many quarters this was received somewhat fatalistically, as the line had never been a money-spinner. In December of that year there were fears that a very abrupt closure might be on the cards as, on the 28th of that month, the bridge over the River Wye at Whitney collapsed; it was widely considered that the BTC would decide not to repair the bridge and that the line would therefore be closed forthwith. However, the repairs *were* sanctioned. While they were being carried out, passengers wishing to travel from, say, Hereford to Brecon were taken by train as far as Eardisley where they had to transfer to a bus; the bus took them to Hay-on-Wye where a train was waiting to take them on to Brecon. The repairs to the bridge were completed with commend-

The Hereford, Hay & Brecon line displayed ample evidence of its pedigree until the very end – despite finishing up as part of the Western Region, the old Midland style fixtures and fittings (right down to the fencing) were retained. From 1953 onwards, even the locomotives were LMSR-designed Ivatt Class 2s. Here, on Friday 10 June 1960, No.46506 is standing at Hay-on-Wye (21¼ miles from Hereford) with the 4.05pm Hereford-Brecon; it is crossing the 4.10pm Brecon-Hereford which is headed by a 'more-WR' form of motive power, namely 0-6-0PT No.3662. It will be noticed that No.46505 carries the 89A shed-plate of Oswestry; the engine was almost certainly based at Brecon but, in November 1959, Brecon had lost its parent shed status and had become a sub of Oswestry, hence the 89A plate. Today, the old station at Hay-on-Wye is one of the few establishments in the area which has not been converted into a bookshop – Hay is, of course, stated to have the largest concentration of second-hand bookshops in the world. And yours truly will be spending a couple of days there later this summer. Whoopee...!! PHOTOGRAPH: HUGH BALLANTYNE

able speed, and it reopened to rail traffic on 15 January 1962.

On Tuesday 24 April 1962 the Hereford-Brecon line was visited by Messrs. R.E.Barby and G.E.Jones, who wrote about their day out in the June 1962 issue of the *Railway Observer*. Messrs. Barby and Jones started their day by travelling on the 9.02am train from Hereford to Brecon which comprised three coaches and was hauled by Ivatt Class 2 No.46508. They noted that permanent way work was in progress near Eardisley – this was in connection with the proposal to retain goods services between Hereford

and Eardisley, thereby making Eardisley a terminus. It was also reported that there was a 15mph speed restriction (complete with flagman) over the Wye Bridge at Whitney. This was a consequence of the bridge collapse the previous December – clearly, the repairs had been of a fairly temporary nature.

Continuing south-westwards, at Talgarth the train crossed the morning pick-up goods from Brecon; this was hauled by another Ivatt Class 2, No.46519. Messrs. Barby and Jones arrived in Brecon on time at 10.44am – it had taken 1 hour 42 minutes to cover the

Moorhampton was 9¼ miles along the line from Hereford. On 6 June 1960 No.46506 arrives at what appears to be the almost deserted station with the 2.15pm from Three Cocks Junction to Hereford. This train had connected at Three Cocks with the 1.20pm Brecon-Moat Lane and the 12.30pm Builth Road-Brecon. PHOTOGRAPH: HUGH BALLANTYNE

38½ miles. Given that the Hereford-Brecon line was hardly the fastest in the land, and that the train had called at twelve of the thirteen intermediate stations (the exception was Groesffordd halt on the Talyllyn Junction-Brecon section), the journey time was not as disastrous as it might seem. Our travellers on 24 April reported that the passenger traffic was 'very thin'.

In all, there were three passenger trains from Hereford to Brecon and four in the opposite direction, but there was an additional train each way between Hereford and Three Cocks Junction (at which latter point they connected with trains on the Mid-Wales Line). By 1962 all trains on the Hereford line were handled from the Brecon end, with the exception of the 9.35am pick-up goods from Hereford (Moorfields) to Three Cocks which was diagrammed for a Hereford engine; Standard Class 2 No.78004 was apparently the usual engine, though a GWR 2251 class 0-6-0 was known to be used on this job on occasions. Previously, the line had also hosted an ICI tank train from Dowlais which had been worked by a pair of Hereford's pannier tanks – the engines brought in empty tank wagons and returned from Dowlais with the full ones, taking them as far as Hereford. However, by 1962 that working had been re-routed via Pontypool Road.

In May 1962 the TUCC approved the proposed withdrawal of passenger services on the Hereford-Brecon line, but it was confirmed that the Hereford-Eardisley section was to be retained for goods traffic, principally to serve customers in the Hay-on-Wye area. The decision to truncate the line at Eardisley instead of Hay-on-Wye itself meant that the bridge over the Wye at Whitney would no longer have to be maintained. The retention of the Hereford-Eardisley section for goods traffic was, however, not regarded as indefinite, as it was anticipated that that section would close completely before too long and that the Hay-on-Wye goods traffic would then be sent by road to or from Hereford.

The withdrawal of the Hereford-Brecon passenger services was set for Monday 31 December 1962. That date was also set for the withdrawal of all other passenger services to Brecon, thereby removing that important market town from the railway map. In the absence of Sunday services, the last public passenger trains ran on Saturday 29 December. The last train on the Hereford line was the 6.00pm from Brecon which was scheduled to arrive at Hereford at 7.40pm; it comprised three coaches and was hauled, somewhat uncharacteristically, by pannier tank No.4627. The return working left Hereford at 9.10pm and was timed to reach Brecon at 10.50pm. This turned out to be the start of one of the worst winters that Wales and the West of England had experienced for many years, and so many enthusiasts found it impossible to visit the area for the 'last day' formalities.

The following day, Sunday 30 December, an SLS special (ten coaches double-headed by a pair of Class 2 2-6-0s) ran through from Brecon to Hereford; the train had arrived at Brecon from Moat Lane. This was, in effect, the 'final farewell'.

As per the earlier proposals, the Hereford-Eardisley section was retained for freight services. These were logically worked by a Hereford engine; during 1963 Standard Class 2 No.78004 was the usual performer, but that engine was transferred away in January 1964 and so a pannier tank was used instead. The freight trips ran three times a week (dep. Hereford 7.35am) and were worked in with a goods trip to Leominster, after which the engine and train went back to Hereford. Before long, the 'three times a week' frequency of the Eardisley trip seemed to be a case of over-provision as, on some occasions, both the outward and return trips ran as engine and brake van only! Inevitably, this did not go unnoticed by BR, and in mid-1964 the withdrawal of services was announced. The formal date of closure was 28 September 1964, but it appears that the last train had actually run a few days earlier.

The final closure of the last section of the old Hereford, Hay & Brecon Railway warranted hardly a mention in the contemporary railway press. But, to be honest, such a low-profile demise was not inappropriate, as the line had spent most of its existence in comparative anonymity.

West Moor station, between Hereford and Credenhill, was a private station, presumably for the benefit of the landowner on whose property the railway was built. Unfortunately, we do not know the date of its closure, but by the time this picture was taken on 6 June 1960, it had clearly been out of use for some considerable time. The train is the 12.42pm Hereford-Three Cocks Junction, hauled by No.46506. PHOTOGRAPH: HUGH BALLANTYNE

Glasbury-on-Wye station was 25¼ miles from Hereford or, to look at things from the other end of the old HHB section, 1½ miles east of Three Cocks. On an unspecified date (but possibly in September 1962 – three months before closure), an Ivatt Class 2 pulls into the station with a train for Hereford. Although the station building appears to be in a good state of repair, the fencing and some of the platform surface seems to have been rather neglected. PHOTOGRAPH: ANDREW MUCKLEY

The Nantlle Railway – branch and tramways
A miscellany, by Bryan L.Wilson and J.Atyeo

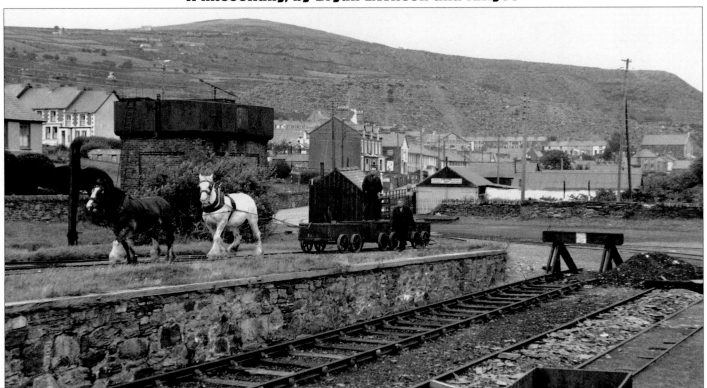

The Vale of Nantlle, six miles in length and roughly in the middle of what used to be Carnarvonshire, lies on an east-west axis, with Rhyd-Ddu (on the Beddgelert-Caernarvon highway) at the eastern end and Pen-y-Groes (on the old Portmadoc-Caernarvon turnpike) at its western end.

Travelling in the area today, one leaves the main Caernarvon-Portmadoc road at Pen-y-Groes and heads east through the Vale to Talysarn which was once the terminus of a standard gauge branch line; but although the terminus was indisputably in the village of Talysarn, it

was named Nantlle after the village 1¼ miles farther east. The journey through the Vale thus far is unspectacular, with the course of the railway roughly following the road; indeed, since the closure of the railway, much of its alignment has actually become the road!

And this is how things were at the other end of the tramway... The eastern extremity of the 3ft 6in gauge Nantlle Railway was at the foot of the double-track inclines which led up to Pen-yr-Orsedd Quarry. Each of the two sections of the incline had its own winding house. At the site of the first winding house, narrow gauge lines crossed from left to right giving access to other levels. PHOTOGTRAPH: C.H.A.TOWNLEY; COURTESY JIM PEDEN/I.R.S.

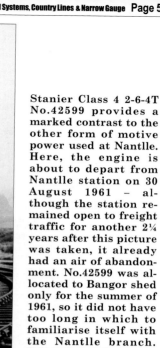

Stanier Class 4 2-6-4T No.42599 provides a marked contrast to the other form of motive power used at Nantlle. Here, the engine is about to depart from Nantlle station on 30 August 1961 – although the station remained open to freight traffic for another 2¼ years after this picture was taken, it already had an air of abandonment. No.42599 was allocated to Bangor shed only for the summer of 1961, so it did not have too long in which to familiarise itself with the Nantlle branch. PHOTOGRAPH: T.J.EDGINGTON

Top left. Transfer traffic at Nantlle station, 5 May 1957. A pair of horses bring three wagons loaded with finished slates into the station. The slate has been transported via the 3ft 6in gauge tramway from the quarries and will be trans-shipped at the station to the standard gauge. The horses are very probably Mr.Oswald Jones's PRINCE and CORWEN; an article in the *Liverpool Daily Post* opined that the equine duo '...are so well trained that they can take empty trucks from the station to the quarry without anyone having to supervise them'. Note the water tank in the background – in much earlier times (certainly prior to 1901) the tank was on the loading dock a little in front of where the horses are seen here. At one time there was a turntable just to the left of the tank, but it was removed in 1901. The 'table was actually used for run-round purposes, the adjacent line of rails also being connected to the table. The standard gauge siding on the near side of the loading dock ends at the buffer stops, but it once extended about ¼-mile eastwards to Coed Madoc Quarry – this was the only quarry in the Vale of Nantlle to be served directly by the standard gauge. The hill in the distance is the 1,138ft-high Mynydd Cilgwyn. PHOTOGRAPH: DAVID LAWRENCE; HUGH DAVIES COLLECTION

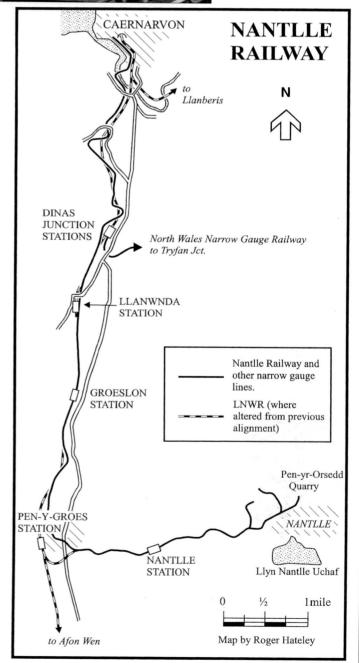

So far, we have passed through a pastoral landscape, but beyond Nantlle station the landscape dramatically changes and we are left in no doubt whatsoever as to why a railway was built here in the first place. The principal reason for the railway's existence was slate and, to the east of the old Nantlle station, we enter another world of old slate quarries and quarrymen's crofts. The quarries were not on the same scale as those at Llanberis or Bethesda, and were certainly not in the 'Blaenau Festiniog' league, but they have nevertheless left a *very* visible mark on the landscape. In fact, they were dug deep in pits along the valley, rather than being carved out from the sides of mountains. Some of the old quarries – parts of Dorothea Quarry, for example – have now filled with water to become lakes.

Further east, beyond Llyn Nantlle Uchaf, Mynydd Mawr (2,290 feet high and known as 'The Elephant' because of its shape) towers above the scree slopes. This part of the Vale remains largely unchanged, and the road runs between rough stone walls to Rhyd Ddu where we

join the Beddgelert road.

The Vale of Nantlle was once the location of one of the two oldest copper mines in Caernarvonshire; this was at Drwys-y-Coed, towards the top of the vale. Cornish miners were at Drwys-y-Coed in 1761, much of the ore being sent to Swansea via the port of Caernarvon. Cilgwyn Quarry near the village of Nantlle is generally recognised as the oldest slate quarry in North Wales. It was revived in the early 19th century, but was surpassed in the 1820s by the better-financed operations at Dinorwic. In the best tradition of the North Wales slate industry, many of the quarries in the Vale of Nantlle were served by a narrow gauge tramway. However, the Nantlle tramway had a rather different history to some of its contemporaries in that, throughout its long life, it was horse-worked. But let it not be thought that a lack of locomotives equates to a lack of interest. Far from it! The Nantlle tramway had a positively fascinating history – not least of all because, despite being a 3ft 6in gauge horse-worked line, it eventually became part of British Railways! – and, as our pictures clearly show, it offered a host of visual delights for railway and industrial enthusiasts, even if the quarrying itself

had not made the kindest of impacts on what had apparently once been a hugely attractive landscape.

.........ooooo00Oooooo.........

There are records of slate extraction at Cilgwyn Quarry in the Vale of Nantlle as early as the 12th century, but it was the early 1800s before the local quarrying industry really took off. That said, as with similar enterprises elsewhere in North Wales, the scope for production in the very early 1800s was initially hampered by poor communications – there was no point in furious extraction at the quarries if the slate could not be transported swiftly and in quantity to the customers. At Penrhyn,

a tramway between the quarries and a new port (Port Penrhyn) had been laid in 1800 and the advantages had quickly become very evident. Somewhat inevitably, the lessees of the quarries in the Nantlle area also turned their thoughts to the laying of a tramway to a point of export. As for the actual point of export, there were only two serious contenders. One was Voryd, a marshy bay at the south-western entrance to the Menai Strait, and the other was Caernarvon. Prior to the development of Port Penrhyn, the long-established port of Caernarvon, despite its shortcomings, had virtually monopolised the export of local slate but, after it had lost a fair proportion of its trade to Port Penrhyn,

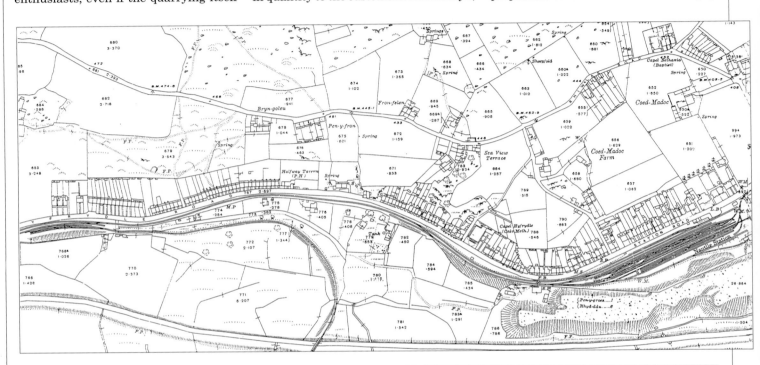

This picture of Nantlle station was almost certainly taken prior to 1901, in which year the station signal box was taken out of use. There are passenger coaches at the left-hand platform, and one of the goods wagons in the foreground is lettered 'M R'. The distinctive signal is a standard LNWR design of 1876 with its lamp positioned below the arm. PHOTOGRAPH: JIM PEDEN COLLECTION

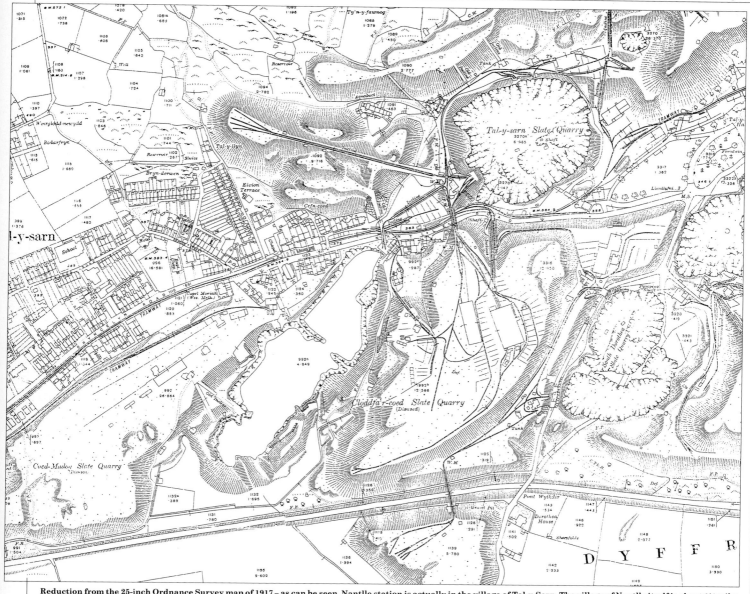

Reduction from the 25-inch Ordnance Survey map of 1917 – as can be seen, Nantlle station is actually in the village of Tal-y-Sarn. The village of Nantlle itself is about 1¼ miles to the east. As mentioned in one of the photo captions, there was once a turntable at the station but it was removed in 1901 – it used to be on what is depicted here as the dead-end road adjacent to the water tower (at the north-east side of the station). This map shows the standard gauge siding extending from the east end of the station to Coed Madoc Quarry which had closed in 1909. A quarter-mile or so to the west of the station, the Caernarvonshire Slate Quarries Tramway diverges from the branch line. This tramway – also 3ft 6in gauge – extended as far as Fron-Heulog Quarry. It is thought to have been in operation from *circa* 1850 until *circa* 1913. The road layout in the Tal-y-Sarn area might seem unfamiliar, but remember that a new road was put through the valley some ten years after this map was drawn. CROWN COPYRIGHT

the Harbour Trustees at Caernarvon were ready to listen to any scheme which might revive their fortunes. Consequently, the trustees enthusiastically allied themselves to the idea of a slate tramway from Nantlle.

On 10 February 1813 a meeting was attended by a number of the major Nantlle lessees, and it was agreed to seek Parliamentary authority to construct a tramway from Nantlle to the Port of Caernarvon. But despite the initial enthusiasm for a tramway, nothing was done to bring the scheme to fruition. Consequently, the Nantlle quarries continued to operate on a comparatively modest scale. However, there was a rude awakening in 1824 when work started on the construction of a tramway between the rapidly expanding Dinorwic Quarries and another new port, the appropriately named Port Dinorwic. With the Penrhyn quarries already having the advantage of their own tramway and port, it was perceived that, with the Dinorwic Quarries following suit, the quarries at Nantlle, with their vastly inferior – and, importantly, more costly – transport arrangements, would be unable to compete.

This finally jerked the Nantlle lessees from their lethargy, and early in 1825 thoughts of a tramway were hastily revived. The Harbour Trustees at Caernarvon were also kick-started into action as the prospect of the Dinorwic slate being diverted to another new port would mean Caernarvon losing much of its remaining business. Things now moved very quickly and, on 18 January 1825, the supporters of the proposed tramway agreed to promote a 'railway or tramroad' starting at or near '…a farm called Talmignedd Issa *(to the east of the village of Nantlle)* situate in the parish of Llanllynfi in the County of Caernarvon and terminating in the town and port of Caernarvon…' with a branch 'terminating in the port and harbour of Voryd'.

The Nantlle Railway Company, as it was formally titled, obtained its Act of Parliament on 20 May 1825. The Act authorised a tramway from '…a certain slate quarry called Gloddfarlon *(about* *halfway between Tal-y-Sarn and Nantlle)* to the Town and Port of Caernarvon'. Clearly, the earlier idea of a branch to Voryd had been dropped. The estimated cost of building the tramway was a little under £19,000 – given the nature of the proposed tramway, this was a very hefty sum indeed. However, the raising of that amount proved to be no problem; no less than £20,000 was subscribed almost at the outset, and so construction work was able to commence almost immediately the Act of Parliament was obtained. The tramway was built to the gauge of 3ft 6in gauge, whereas many other slate tramways in North Wales were built to a gauge of 2ft or slightly less. The advantage of the 3ft 6in gauge over the 2ft gauge was that heavier loads could be carried with little increase in haulage or maintenance costs, but there was a disadvantage – in theory, at least. Although each of the North Wales slate tramways operated in isolation – in other words there were virtually no instances of interchange between individual railways – the alternative of a 'popular' gauge might

Memorandum of Association
OF THE

NANTLLE UNITED QUARRIES COMPANY,
LIMITED.

I. The name of the Company is the NANTLLE UNITED QUARRIES COMPANY, LIMITED.

II. The Registered Office of the Company will be situate in England.

III. The objects for which the Company is established are :

(a) To acquire the lease of the quarries, veins, beds or strata of slate or slate rock in, under and throughout the lands known as Dolwenith Penralt Goch, part of Nant Nova and Cyllydyart (except any common land), in the County of Carnavon, containing about 50 acres, dated the 30th June, 1887, whereby the said premises are held for a term of 42 years from the 25th May, 1885, at the rent and royalties therein mentioned.

(b) To acquire the lease of the quarries, veins, beds or strata of slate or slate rock, in and under the lands known as Taleithin Uchaf Caerwaen and part of Nant Nova (except any common land), situate in the County of Carnarvon, and containing together 76 acres, 3 roods, 33 perches, or thereabouts, bearing the same date and made for the same term as the last mentioned lease.

(c) To acquire the lease of the quarries, rocks, and beds of slate, stones, slabs, flags and other stones within, under or upon the several closes or parcels of land, part of a farm called Tyddyn Agnes, situate in the parish of Llanllyfni, in the County of Carnarvon, containing about 32 acres, dated the 10th April, 1874, whereby the said premises are held for 21 years from the 1st November, 1873, at the rent and royalties therein mentioned.

von; these were, or course, horse-worked. Preston's activities were unpopular among the quarry lessees at Nantlle. The general disquiet among the lessees was because Preston seemed to be building up the passenger service at the expense of the slate traffic – indeed, it was alleged that Preston had lifted a number of the sidings where slate trains had been in the habit of passing. The over-riding suspicion was that Preston had an eye to the future – it looked likely that a standard gauge passenger-carrying railway would eventually penetrate southwards from Caernarvon and, if that were to happen, the company concerned might be prepared to pay a disproportionately high price for the little Nantlle Railway. Edward Preston would, of course, do rather well from a sell-out.

A standard gauge passenger railway *did* eventually penetrate southwards from Caernarvon, but not until the latter part of the 1860s. Edward Preston was still on the scene at the time – he still leased the Nantlle Railway – but it seems that he had less ability to pull any important strings. The Carnarvonshire Railway (note the spelling) was authorised in July 1862 to build an 18¾-mile long line from Caernarvon to Afon Wen, at which latter point it would form a junction with the Aberystwyth & Welsh Coast Railway's Portmadoc-Pwllheli line. The Carnarvonshire Railway Company was aware that, between Caernarvon and Pen-y-Groes, its line would duplicate that of the Nantlle Railway. Although consideration was initially given to building a duplicate line, the Carnarvonshire company later abandoned that idea and, instead, courted the Nantlle Railway with a view to taking over the latter's line and reconstructing it to the standard gauge for use by locomotive-hauled passenger trains. The courtship bore fruit and, on 25 July 1867, the Nantlle Railway was formally

have least enabled rolling stock etc to be built to 'standard' narrow gauge designs. On the Nantlle Tramway, the rails were of iron and weighed a mere 16lbs per yard; the chairs in which they were carried were laid on stone blocks.

The tramway opens
The Nantlle Railway was formally opened for freight traffic on 12 July 1828. It extended for a distance of 9¼ miles from Gloddfarlon Quarry (referred to at the time as Gloddfa'r Lon Slate Quarries) to Caernarvon Quay. It appears that the method of operation was for the proprietors of the quarries to individually provide their own horse-power. The coming of the railway had a marked effect in the Nantlle area as the larger, rail-connected

quarries became busier than ever, while a number of the smaller workings saw their trade decline. But the railway itself was a success and, by the late 1840s, was handling around 20,000 tons of slate per year and returning an annual profit in the region of £2,500.

However, despite the railway's success, in July 1856 the proprietors agreed to it being leased by one Edward Preston for £2,000 p.a., rising in yearly increments to £2,500. Preston's background was the subject of some speculation; he professed to be a railway engineer, but it was later suggested that he was actually a pawn of the Chester & Holyhead Railway. On 11 August 1856 – only weeks after the commencement of his lease – Preston introduced a passenger service of four trains each day between Nantlle and Caernar-

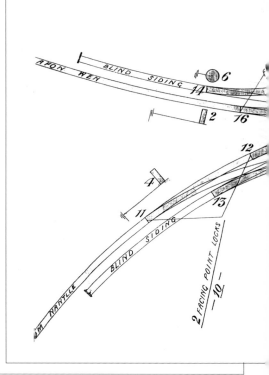

The sturdy, but somewhat neglected, station building at Nantlle was photographed on 30 August 1961, almost thirty years after it had last been regularly used by railway passengers. Nevertheless, it had clearly been put to good use – the sign near the door reads 'Clwb y Wydffa' which, of course, means the Snowdon Club. The standard gauge track is almost completely obscured by the 3ft 6in gauge loading dock, from which this picture was taken. Looking again at the sign above the door... The use of the Welsh language on the sign confirms that, in this part of the world, the native tongue has always been prominent – it is not just latter-day political correctness or a rose-tinted yearning for traditionalism. Welsh is the main language for many folk in Caernarvonshire, and not too many years ago it was the *only* language. This could create a problem or two – for example, on 17 December 1868 the L&NWR Traffic Committee discussed a request from the Station Master at Bangor that the company rule book *'...should be printed in Welsh for the benefit of men who cannot read English'*. The L&NWR's response was blunt: *'In future, no Welshman to be appointed to a responsible post who cannot read and write English, and that men now employed for whom the rule book is proposed to be translated, are to be informed that they must learn to read and speak English to entitle them to remain in the service'*. That was over 130 years ago, but some say that Euston *still* does not understand North Wales... PHOTOGRAPH: T.J.EDGINGTON

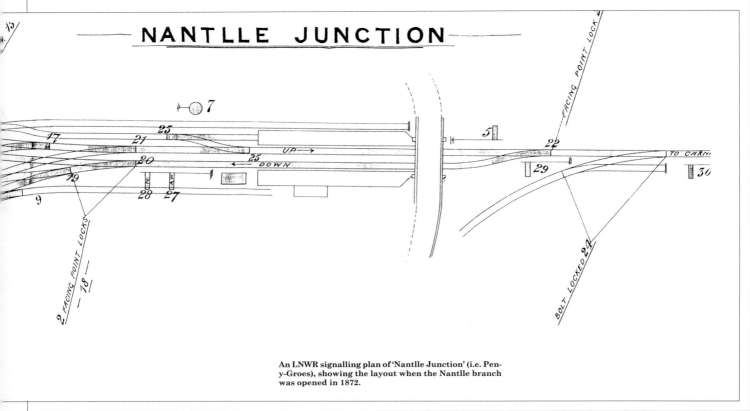

An LNWR signalling plan of 'Nantlle Junction' (i.e. Pen-y-Groes), showing the layout when the Nantlle branch was opened in 1872.

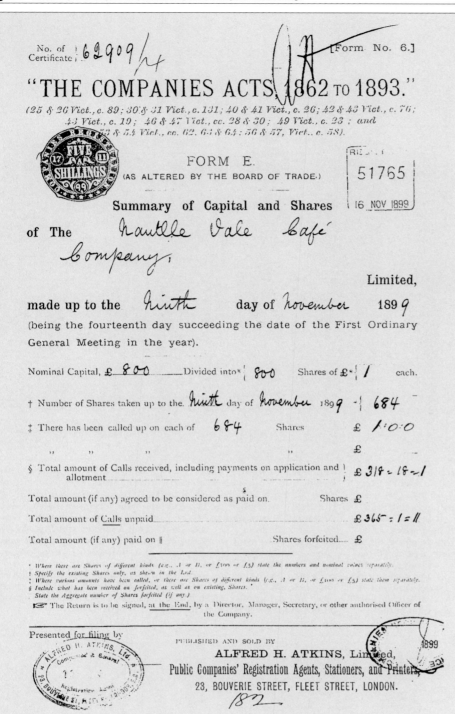

No. of Certificate : **62909/4**

[Form No. 6.]

"THE COMPANIES ACTS, 1862 TO 1893."

(25 & 26 Vict., c. 89 ; 30 & 31 Vict., c. 131 ; 40 & 41 Vict., c. 26 ; 42 & 43 Vict., c. 76 ;
43 Vict., c. 19 ; 46 & 47 Vict., cc. 28 & 30 ; 49 Vict., c. 23 ; and
53 & 54 Vict., cc. 62, 63 & 64 ; 56 & 57, Vict., c. 58).

FORM E.
(AS ALTERED BY THE BOARD OF TRADE.)

51765

16 NOV 1899

Summary of Capital and Shares

of The **Nantlle Vale Café Company,**

Limited,

made up to the **ninth** day of **November** 189**9**

(being the fourteenth day succeeding the date of the First Ordinary General Meeting in the year).

Nominal Capital, £ **800** Divided into* **800** Shares of £* **1** each.

† Number of Shares taken up to the **ninth** day of **November** 189**9** **684**

‡ There has been called up on each of **684** Shares £ **1·0·0**

" " " " £

" " " " £

§ Total amount of Calls received, including payments on application and allotment £ **318 = 18 = 1**

Total amount (if any) agreed to be considered as paid on. Shares £

Total amount of Calls unpaid £ **365 = 1 = 11**

Total amount (if any) paid on ‖ Shares forfeited...... £

* Where there are Shares of different kinds (e.g. A or B, or £100 or £5) state the numbers and nominal values separately.
† Specify the existing Shares only, as shewn in the List.
‡ Where various amounts have been called, or there are Shares of different kinds (e.g. A or B, or £100 or £5) state them separately.
§ Include what has been received on forfeited, as well as on existing Shares.
‖ State the Aggregate number of Shares forfeited (if any.)

☞ The Return is to be signed, at the End, by a Director, Manager, Secretary, or other authorised Officer of the Company.

Presented for filing by

PUBLISHED AND SOLD BY

ALFRED H. ATKINS, Limited,
Public Companies' Registration Agents, Stationers, and Printers,
23, BOUVERIE STREET, FLEET STREET, LONDON.

---

vested in the Carnarvonshire Railway Company.

The idea of reconstructing the Nantlle Railway to the standard gauge had, in fact, been under consideration since 1864, and traffic on the railway had been interrupted on several occasions in 1864-66 so that certain works could be undertaken. The passenger trains on the Nantlle Railway had ceased on 10 June 1865, and on 6 August 1866 – i.e. the year prior to the amalgamation with the Carnarvonshire Railway – the horse-worked traffic between Tyddyn Bengam (just to the north of Pen-y-Groes) and Coed Helen (on the south bank of the River Seiont in Caernarvon) had been completely suspended in preparation for major reconstruction.

The reconstruction included four deviations from the original alignment: one at Pen-y-Groes, one just to the north of Tyddyn Bengam, one to facilitate the construction of Llanwnda passenger station (this station is stated to have owed its existence more to the proximity of the Glyn Lifon estate rather than the few houses in the village), and a two-mile deviation on a somewhat straighter alignment to the north of the site of Dinas station. This effectively divided the old Nantlle Railway into three sections:
• The standard gauge section (see above), a total distance of approximately 5 miles.
• The section between Coed Helen and the quays at Caernarvon Harbour; this section retained the 3ft 6in gauge and continued to be worked by horses.
• The 3-mile long section between Tyddyn Bengam and the quarries, which remained as a 3ft 6in gauge horse-worked line with interchange facilities at Tyddyn Bengam. The Carnarvonshire Railway had earlier proposed a standard gauge branch line from Pen-y-Groes to Nantlle, but that proposal had fallen by the wayside.

The line from Caernarvon through to Afon Wen was formally opened as a standard gauge locomotive worked line on 2 September 1867. That said, the first use of locomotives on the line had been on 6 August 1866 and, during that very same summer, at least four locomotive-worked excursion trains had run from Caernarvon to Portmadoc or Barmouth. That, however, had been highly unofficial and,

The Nantlle branch joined the Caernarvon-Afon Wen branch at Pen-y-Groes, where this picture was taken on 30 August 1961. We are looking northwards towards Caernarvon – the Nantlle branch diverges to the right behind the photographer. The bay which was used by the Nantlle branch passenger trains is behind the down (right-hand) platform – unfortunately, it is almost completely obscured here. Pen-y-Groes signal box worked with Groeslon and Brynkir boxes on the Afon Wen line and also controlled the Nantlle branch; it was a Saxby & Farmer box with a tumbler frame which, according to an L&NWR signalling plan of 1897, had 29 working levers and 4 spare. The box closed on 7 December 1964. Note that the down platform is signalled for two-way working. PHOTOGRAPH: T.J.EDGINGTON

Cynics might say that an article about a North Wales location would hardly be complete without a show of mist and drizzle. This 'not-unusual' weather scene shows Nantlle station on 14 November 1952. PHOTOGRAPH: HUGH BALLANTYNE

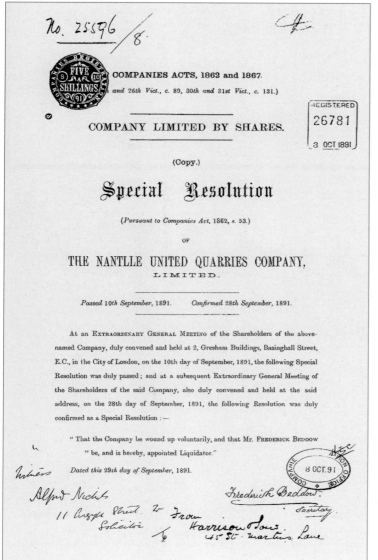

somehow, had managed to escape the Board of Trade's attention until an accident occurred.

The owner of the line, the Carnarvonshire Railway, soon came to enjoy a level of self-sufficiency as, from the summer of 1868, it was able to boast its own locomotives and rolling stock (although some of the stock was actually on loan or hired). However, the self-sufficiency and independence did not last for very long as, on 4 July 1870, the company was taken over by the L&NWR. Prior to the L&NWR take-over the passenger terminus at the Caernarvon end of the railway was Pant

Station, on the west bank of the Afon Seiont, but shortly after the take-over, the Caernarvon-Afon Wen trains started using the L&NWR station at Caernarvon, and the station at Pant was therefore closed.

Not altogether surprisingly, the proprietors of the quarries at Nantlle were less than happy with the new arrangements on the Caernarvon-Afon Wen line. As the Nantlle branch and the Caernarvon Quay section were still 3ft 6in gauge horse-worked lines, there were two breaks of gauge – goods going from Nantlle to Caernarvon had to be trans-shipped from narrow gauge to standard gauge at Tyddyn Bengam and back from standard gauge to narrow gauge at Coed Helen. The quarry proprietors claimed that they had had to increase their wagon stock by 25% because of the delays caused by trans-shipping, and it was also claimed that the additional man-handling resulted in a far greater number of breakages. There were also other grumbles; Mr.Derbyshire, the superintendent of Pen-yr-Orsedd Quarry, complained that: '...with regard to hay for the horses, it has been pilfered to the extent of 4cwts out of a ton, so that it is no longer economical to bring it by train from Carnarvon Market'. Mr.Darbyshire also noted that: '...the transport of timber now costs 8/4d per ton, whereas it used to cost only 3/2¾d when the 3ft 6in gauge existed throughout'. The Mayor of Caernarvon complained that the cessation of through passenger workings from Nantlle to Caernarvon was '...injurious to the trade of the town as well as a hardship to the residents adjacent to the Nantlle Railway'. The complainants pressed for the reinstatement of the 3ft 6in gauge right

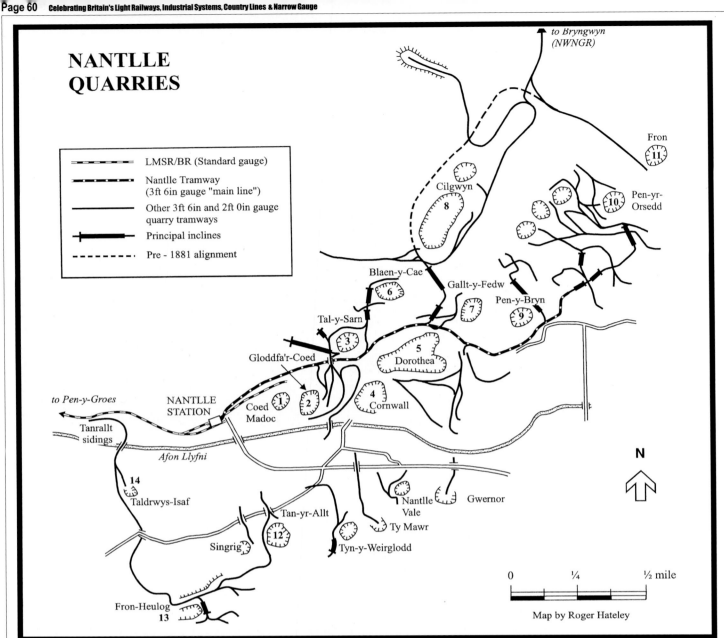

NANTLLE QUARRIES

to Bryngwyn (NWNGR)

	LMSR/BR (Standard gauge)
	Nantlle Tramway (3ft 6in gauge "main line")
	Other 3ft 6in and 2ft 0in gauge quarry tramways
	Principal inclines
	Pre - 1881 alignment

Fron
(11)

Cilgwyn
(8)

Pen-yr-Orsedd
(10)

Blaen-y-Cae
(6)

Gallt-y-Fedw
(7)

Pen-y-Bryn
(9)

Tal-y-Sarn
(3)

Dorothea
(5)

Gloddfa'r-Coed

Coed Madoc
(1) (2)

Cornwall
(4)

to Pen-y-Groes

NANTLLE STATION

Tanrallt sidings

Afon Llyfni

(14)
Taldrwys-Isaf

Tan-yr-Allt

Singrig

(12)

Tyn-y-Weirglodd

Nantlle Vale

Gwernor

Ty Mawr

N

Fron-Heulog
13

| 0 | ¼ | ½ mile |

Map by Roger Hateley

Looking westwards from the trans-shipment dock at Nantlle station on a wet and dismal 14 November 1952. Note the simple, but perfectly effective, 'moveable diamonds' where the 3ft 6in gauge rails cross each other. PHOTOGRAPH: HUGH BALLANTYNE

VALE OF NANTLLE – slate quarries connected to the Nantlle Railway
Most details gleaned from *Narrow Gauge Railways in North Caernarvonshire, Vol.3*, by J.I.C.Boyd

No. on map	Name of quarry	Dates working	Internal railway(s)	Notes
1	Coed Madoc (Gloddfa'r-Glai)	pre-1820 to 1909 *	Std. gauge siding from Nantlle stn; 2ft gauge in quarries; locomotives used c.1880-1900s	
2	Gloddfa'r-Coed (Bangor & Caernarvon)	1790 to c.1940 *	2ft and 3ft 6in gauge; non-locomotive	
3	Tal-y-Sarn	1802 to c.1930 *	2ft and 3ft 6in gauge; locomotives used c.1878-c.1915	(a)
4	Cornwall (South Dorothea)	1867 to 1937 *	3ft 6in gauge; non-locomotive	
5	Dorothea (Gloddfa'r-Turner)	c.1829 to 1970	2ft gauge; locomotives used c.1870-c.1970	(b)
6	Blaen-y-Cae	c.1870 to 1931 *	2ft and 3ft 6in gauge; non-locomotive	
7	Gallt-y-Fedw (Victoria or Alexandria)	c.1857 to 1937 *	2ft and 3ft 6in gauge; non-locomotive	
8	Cilgwyn	c.1800 to 1956 *	2ft and 3ft 6in gauge; locomotives used 1876-c.1939	(c), (d)
9	Pen-y-Bryn (*inc.* Gloddfa'r-Lon)	c.1770 to 1892 *	2ft and 3ft 6in gauge; locomotives used 1875-1892	(e)
10	Pen-yr-Orsedd	1816 to 1979	2ft and 3ft 6in gauge; locomotives used c.1877-1970	(f)
11	Fron	c.1815 to 1950 *	2ft and 3ft 6in gauge; locomotives used c.1878-c.1915	(g), (h)
12	Tan-yr-Allt ('Caernarvonshire Slate')	1805 to 1930 *	3ft 6in gauge; non-locomotive	(j)
13	Fron-Heulog	c.1840 to 1913 *	3ft 6in gauge; non-locomotive	
14	Taldrws-Isaf	1859 to 1870	small internal non-locomotive tramway system; believed to be 2ft gauge	

* Period of working NOT continuous
(a) Eventually comprised three quarries
(b) Road haulage used from *circa* 1963
(c) Eventually incorporated four other quarries
(d) Connected to North Wales Narrow Gauge Railway in the early 1920s
(e) Comprised four quarries, known collectively as Pen-y-Bryn
(f) Road tractor haulage used after cessation of locomotive working
(g) Only intermittent small-scale working after 1915
(h) Connected to North Wales Narrow Gauge Railway in 1881
(j) Ceased to use Nantlle Railway in 1879

opened to freight traffic on 22 May 1872, and the remaining mile to 'Nantlle' on 1 August 1872. (Note the inverted commas for 'Nantlle' – although the branch terminus was named Nantlle, that station was very firmly in the village of Tal-y-Sarn, some 1¼ miles west of the village of Nantlle itself).

Early in September 1872 the branch was inspected for the Board of Trade; this was an essential prelude to opening the line for public passenger traffic. The inspecting officer, Colonel Rich, reported on 9 September 1872: *'The new line is 1 mile 34 chains in length. The permanent way consists of double-headed rail that weighs 75lbs per lineal yard. The line is well ballasted with gravel. The steepest gradient is 1 in 62 and the sharpest curve has a radius of 7½ chains. There are no public level crossings; a turntable has been provided at Nantlle. The junctions of the several sidings at Nantlle and Tanrallt are worked from raised cabins…'.* Colonel Rich was unhappy about various aspects of the interlocking, and declined to 'pass' the line for opening. The necessary alterations were, however, soon carried out, and the branch formally opened to public passenger traffic on 1 October 1872.

The old 3ft 6in gauge was retained beyond the passenger terminus to the quarries, while most of the internal lines at the quarries themselves were 2ft (nominal) gauge. In places, the two gauges ran together as a 'three-rail' layout. The Nantlle branch settled down to a routine existence which was to remain substantially unchanged for almost sixty years. The branch was worked on the 'one engine in steam' principle and, following the clo-

through from Nantlle to Caernarvon, with 2ft (nominal) adopted as standard in the quarries, but the Board of Trade, acting as referee, opined that the best solution all round would be firstly, for the standard gauge to replace the 3ft 6in gauge at the Caernarvon end; secondly, for the standard gauge to be extended from Pen-y-Groes to Nantlle, at which latter point a new trans-shipment depot should be

provided and, thirdly, for passenger services to be operated on the Pen-y-Groes-Nantlle section. The alterations recommended by the Board of Trade were soon carried out by the L&NWR.

L&NWR days
It appears that the first half-mile of the 'new' locomotive-worked standard gauge line between Pen-y-Groes and 'Nantlle'

In May 1957, a fair number of unfitted vans were stored in the sidings at Nantlle, while on the 3ft 6in gauge, a pair of 2-ton capacity slate wagons are clearly marked *NOT TO GO*. PHOTOGRAPH: DOUGLAS ROBINSON

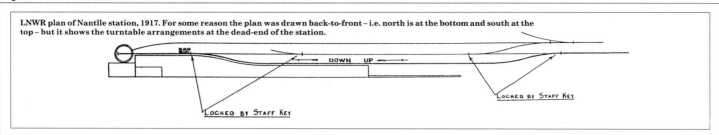

LNWR plan of Nantlle station, 1917. For some reason the plan was drawn back-to-front – i.e. north is at the bottom and south at the top – but it shows the turntable arrangements at the dead-end of the station.

After leaving the station yard at Nantlle, the tramway crossed the 'new' Nantlle road (the one which was laid in the mid-1920s – this is going off right) at the point where it joined the 'old' Nantlle road (the one heading off in the distance). As is evident, the track across the road had a check rail on both sides – this was because the wheels of the tramway wagons had flanges on both sides. This picture was taken on 2 April 1959. PHOTOGRAPH: JIM PEDEN

sure of Nantlle signal box *circa* 1901 there were no signals on the line except for fixed distants at Tynyweirglodd Level Crossing. (The Board of Trade inspection report of 1867 stated that the line had no level crossings, and so Tynyweirglodd Crossing had clearly been a later addition). The usual practice in the early 1900s was for the first and last trains of the day

to work through to/from Caernarvon, but the other branch trains started and terminated at Pen-y-Groes where they used the bay platform. The trains were usually formed of ordinary 6-wheeeled L&NWR carriages. In terms of passenger revenue, the Nantlle branch was never likely to be the world's greatest money-spinner and, in an attempt to reduce op-

erating costs, in 1912 the L&NWR introduced steam railmotor workings on the line. It appears that the railmotors were taken off *circa* 1914 and replaced by locomotive-hauled trains. This was a consequence of the slate traffic being busy at the time; there were sometimes more slate wagons at Nantlle than the branch goods engine could manage in the time

Continuing eastwards from Nantlle station, the tramway threaded its way through the village of Tal-y-Sarn, running parallel to Bryncelyn Road. At one point it passed through a short tunnel underneath a couple of houses and the steps to the chapel. This picture was taken on 28 April 1957 and, judging by the cluster of gabardine-clad young men(whose presence seems to be causing some concern to the little terrier!), this was very probably the day of an enthusiasts' railtour. PHOTOGRAPH: C.H.A.TOWNLEY; COURTESY JIM PEDEN/I.R.S.

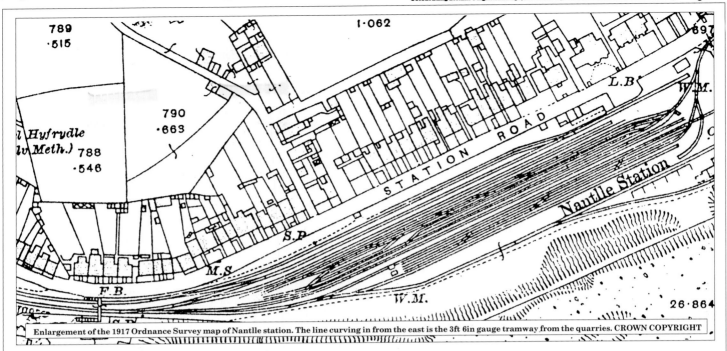

Enlargement of the 1917 Ordnance Survey map of Nantlle station. The line curving in from the east is the 3ft 6in gauge tramway from the quarries. CROWN COPYRIGHT

allotted, but a branch passenger engine could always be called on to help out – this was not possible with a railmotor. The usual practice at this time was for the wagons from the Nantlle branch to be made into full trains at Pen-y-Groes.

During World War I a petrol-engined railcar was tried on the branch. Unfortunately, little seems to be known about this unusual machine, but it seems to have been woefully unsuccessful – as one observer put it, it couldn't pull, it couldn't shunt, and it froze in winter.

The WTT for the Nantlle branch for the summer of 1916 shows a mix of motor trains and ordinary 'hauled' trains. The pattern of working in 1916 was for the branch engine to leave Caernarvon in the morning assisting an Afon Wen train (except on Monday mornings when it took the passenger stock). At the end of the day, the branch engine took any odd wagons back to Caernarvon, and at weekends it took the coaches back for cleaning.

The branch passenger services were suspended as a wartime economy on 1 January 1917 (this also happened on a number of other branches elsewhere in Britain), but were not reinstated until 5 May 1919.

As for freight, the slate traffic inevitably had its peaks and troughs. At the quarries themselves, the 2ft gauge lines were laid, lifted or repositioned as required. Given the landscape at the quarries, the extensive use of the 2ft gauge there was almost inevitable, but it meant that slate had to be trans-shipped to the 3ft 6in gauge for transportation to Nantlle, where it had to be trans-shipped again to the standard gauge. Although the use of 'piggy back' transporter wagons was fairly common in the North Wales slate industry (these were standard gauge wagons on which narrow gauge wagons could be carried), and although the L&NWR itself had transporter wagons, this mode of transportation was not employed at

The 'main line' of the Nantlle Tramway skirted the north side of Dorothea Quarry, passing through an arch underneath an old incline. The old incline is long since disused – a small tree is growing near its foot! – and, as far as we can make out, there are no rails left on it. Crumpled wagons and a winding wheel lie in a heap alongside the bottom of the incline. The date is 28 April 1957. PHOTOGRAPH: C.H.A.TOWNLEY; COURTESY JIM PEDEN/I.R.S.

NANTLLE BRANCH – Single Line. (One class only).
Train Staff Stations – Penygroes and Nantlle.

Miles	WEEK-DAYS DOWN	1 Goods	2 Conveys empty Motor	3	4 Pass	5	6 Empt Motor	7	8 Motor	9	10 Motor	11	12	13	14 Motor	15
		a.m.			a.m.		a.m.		a.m.		p.m.				p.m.	
½	PEN-Y-GROES dep	8 30		...	9 50	...	11 20	...	11 50	...	1 10	...	...	...	3 5	
	Tanrhallt Siding ...	X														
1	NANTLLE arr	8 40		...	9 55	...	11 25	...	11 55	...	1 15	...		...	3 10	

	WEEK-DAYS DOWN	16	17 Motor	18	19	20	21 Motor SO	22	23	24 Motor	25	26	27	28	29 Motor	30
			p.m.				p.m			p.m.					p.m.	
	PEN-Y-GROES dep	a.	6 5	...			7 35		...	8 10	...				8 40	...
	Tanrhallt Siding	...							...							
	NANTLLE arr		6 10	...			7 40		...	8 15	...				8 45	...

Miles	WEEK-DAYS UP	31	32 Pass	33	34 Goods	35	36 Motor	37	38	39 Motor	40	41	42	43	44 Motor	45
			a.m.		a.m.	Conveys empty Motor	a.m.			p.m.					p.m.	
	NANTLLE dep	...	9 30	...	10 50		11 30	...	...	12 50	...				2 20	...
	Tanrhallt Siding	...			...				...							
1	PEN-Y-GROES arr	...	9 35	...	11 0		11 35	...	...	12 55	...				2 25	...

	WEEK-DAYS UP	46	47 Motor	48	49 Motor SO	50	51 Motor	52	53	54 Motor	55	56	57 Empt Motor	58	59	60
			p.m.		p.m.		p.m.			p.m.			p.m.			
	NANTLLE dep	...	4 40	...	7 15	...	7 50	...	...	8 20	...		8 50	...	...	...
	Tanrhallt Siding	...			...			...								
	PEN-Y-GROES arr	...	4 45	...	7 20		7 55	...	...	8 25	...		8 55	...		...

No. 1—Engine works Nos. 4 and 32.

Working timetable, 4 July 1916 until further notice.

Nantlle. The problem seems to have been that of accommodating an adequate (i.e. economical) number of 3ft 6in gauge wagons on the standard gauge transporters.

The only rail-connected quarry at Nantlle that was unaffected by these breaks of gauge was Coed Madoc Quarry – it had the unique luxury of a standard gauge siding directly to Nantlle goods yard. The siding was L&NWR property.

Inevitably, a number of the quarries changed owners, while others ceased working. Those which had ceased working had not necessarily done so because of a lack of slate – the reason for closure was often that they had nowhere left in which to tip the spoil or, alternatively, inadequate drainage. The problem of where to tip the spoil was such that, at one time, there were thoughts of building a tramway westwards from Tal-y-Sarn so that spoil could be taken to the coast for tipping, but this scheme did not come to fruition. As for drainage, this problem was slightly eased in the mid-1890s by the realignment and deepening of the Afon Llynfi which flowed through the Vale of Nantlle.

Post-Grouping

At the Grouping in 1923, the L&NWR became part and parcel of the LMSR. The old 3ft 6in gauge Nantlle tramway also became LMSR property. In early LMSR days, the passenger services on the Nantlle branch comprised eleven down trains and twelve up (weekdays only, of course). Of these trains, one in each direction worked through to/from Caernarvon; most of the others were timed to connect with trains between Caernarvon and Afon Wen. There was also an unadvertised late evening train from Bangor to Nantlle on Saturdays; it was timed to leave Bangor at 9.20pm and arrive at Nantlle at 10.28pm, after which the engine and empty stock returned to Caernarvon. The ordinary branch trains were usually single-coach push-pull sets which offered only Third Class accommodation. The usual locomotives were L&NWR Coal Tanks (the famous Webb 0-6-2Ts).

On the freight side, by the early 1920s the output of the quarries in the Vale of Nantlle had dropped considerably but, because of the very poor road communications in the Vale, the majority of it was still dispatched by rail. That said, not all of the rail-borne traffic went via the Nantlle branch as, in 1923, Cilgwyn Quarry (a significant source of traffic) started dispatching its slate via the Bryngwyn branch of the North Wales Narrow Gauge Railway. Some other quarries in the Moel Tryfan part of the Vale also used the North Wales Narrow Gauge. However, the almost total dependence on

Here we are looking west on 28 April 1957; Pen-yr-Orsedd Quarry is some way behind the photographer, and the 'main line' of the tramway branches off to the right to continue towards Nantlle station. The line continuing straight ahead is part of the original alignment of the Nantlle Tramway, but part of that route was swallowed up by the expansion of Dorothea Quarry, hence the new alignment. PHOTOGRAPH: C.H.A.TOWNLEY; COURTESY JIM PEDEN/I.R.S.

Dorothea Quarry, May 1964. The 1ft 11½in (nominal 2ft) gauge was still in use at the quarry at this time, but the connection to the Nantlle Tramway (through the arch on the right) had been lifted. The trackwork at the points in the foreground is interesting – two lengths of rail could be physically lifted out and positioned as required; this method of operation might sound remarkably primitive, but the options were actually rather limited as the tramway wagons had double-flanged wheels. PHOTOGRAPH: C.H.A.TOWNLEY; COURTESY JIM PEDEN/I.R.S.

rail transport – be it the Nantlle branch or the North Wales Narrow Gauge – changed in 1927 when a new road (later designated the B4418) was opened through the Vale of Nantlle.

The opening of the new road coincided with a down-turn in the fortunes of the local quarrying industry, partly due to the aftermath of the General Strike. These factors resulted in a reduction in, not only

the slate traffic on the Nantlle branch, but also the passenger traffic. By the early 1930s the passenger traffic was negligible (during the whole of 1931, passenger train receipts were just £248) and so it

On its approach to Tal-y-Sarn Quarry from the west, the Nantlle Tramway passed beneath a massive wall which was crossed by the tramway between Tal-y-Sarn Quarry (off left) and Cornwall Quarry (off right). The high-level tramway was locomotive worked and, in 1879, a locomotive fell off the line and on to the tramway below. The larger arch on the right is over a road which, prior to the construction of the new road through the Vale of Nantlle in the late 1920s, was the main road – comparatively speaking! – between the villages of Tal-y-Sarn and Nantlle. This picture was taken on 2 April 1959. PHOTOGRAPH: JIM PEDEN

NANTLLE BRANCH (L.& N.W.) - NORTH WALES).
Proposed withdrawal of passenger train service.

        The Chief General Superintendent reported
that the receipts from passenger traffic on the Nantlle Branch
have decreased in recent years, the total value of the
passenger traffic to and from the Branch for the year 1931
being £248. With a view to effecting economy, and after
consultation with the Solicitor, it was recommended, with the
approval of the Executive, that the passenger train service
be withdrawn and Nantlle Station be closed for passenger
traffic as from the 8th August, 1932.

        It is proposed to continue the freight
train facilities on the Branch, the traffic for the year 1931
amounting to 28,921 tons and £21,850 receipts.

        Parcels and miscellaneous traffic would
continue to be dealt with at Nantlle, such traffic being
conveyed by the Goods Department road motor at present operating between Penygroes and Nantlle.

        The branch line is worked in accordance
with Appendix III of the Book of Rules and Regulations (one
engine in steam). No alterations in the permanent way
or signalling are proposed, but it is recommended that the
existing level crossing gates at Tynyweirglodd crossing,
which do not fence the railway when opened for road traffic,
be substituted by gates as shewn on plan No.51082, which,
with the alterations indicated thereon at a total estimated
cost of £95 (Revenue) would enable the services of the
Crossing Keeper to be dispensed with.

        It is estimated that the carrying out
of the proposal will result in a net annual economy of
£1,254 made up as follows :-

	Per annum.
Savings in staff, loco. running expenses, etc. ...	£1,405.
Estimated loss in receipts ...	151.
Net economy	£1,254.

Approved, and
Ordered accordingly.   LMS Traffic Committee, 22 June 1932.

came as little surprise when it was announced that the passenger services were
to be withdrawn. The official date of their
withdrawal was Monday 8 August 1932
but, in the absence of a Sunday service,
the last public trains ran the previous Saturday, the 6th.

Despite the with-
drawal of passen-
ger services, there
was no question
that the Nantlle
branch should close
completely. As can
be seen, during
1931 it handled
28,921 tons of
freight which gener-
ated receipts of
£21,850 – these fig-
ures were rather
healthy, and more
or less ensured the
branch's retention
for freight. Never-
theless, the local
slate industry
steadily contracted
and, by 1939 only
two of the quarries
connected to the
Nantlle Railway
remained perma-
nently operational:
Dorothea Quarry
(with a staff of over
300) and Pen-yr-
Orsedd Quarry (with its own 2ft gauge
locomotive-worked system). After World
War II, there was a much increased de-
mand for roofing slate to repair war-time
damage and for general rebuilding, and
the combined output from the quarries
required four horse-worked trips to and
from Nantlle station each weekday, with
some of the trips involving up to fifteen
wagons being drawn by a team of horses.
Adhering to long-established practice, the
horse-working was contracted out to local
hauliers. That said, since 1930 all the
work had been undertaken by just one
family concern; this was the Jones family
of Tal-y-Sarn – the father, William Jones,
eventually passed the business to his son,
Oswald.

State ownership

With the birth of British Railways on 1
January 1948, the Nantlle branch became
part of the London Midland Region. Somewhat anachronistically, the 3ft 6in gauge
horse-worked tramway between Nantlle
station and the quarries also became
LMR property. The horse working was
still contracted to Oswald Jones – this
was a very early (not to mention rare) example of non-BR motive power being used
on a BR-owned line!

The LMR Working Timetables for the
summer of 1950 listed only one freight
train on the Nantlle branch on Mondays
to Fridays. It was scheduled to leave
Menai Bridge Yard (at Menai Bridge station) at 7.30am and, after calling at Caernarvon, Dinas, Llanwnda (if required),
Tudor Siding and Pen-y-Groes, it was
timed to reach Nantlle at 10.35am. The
return working left Nantlle for Menai
Bridge Yard at 12.35pm. The usual engines were Stanier 4MT 2-6-4Ts or 4F
0-6-0s.

During the summer of 1955 Nantlle saw its first regular passenger workings for over twenty years. That said, these were not ordinary scheduled trains and, furthermore, they were 'one way only'. This reprise involved weekend excursions to Rhyl – the outbound train each Saturday started from Pen-y-Groes, but the return train continued to Nantlle, arriving a little after midnight.

Returning to the matter of freight workings, as the 1950s progressed the slate traffic declined. This was reflected by the fact that, in 1956, the Nantlle branch freight services were cut back to three trips per week. On the 3ft 6in gauge

Below. 'Workshop Level', Pen-yr-Orsedd Quarry, May 1964. The 'inverted CND' symbol on the side of the wagon denotes that it is the property of Pen-yr-Orsedd; at one time, the use of symbols on railway equipment and stock was commonplace (not only on the Nantlle Tramway but on all manner of railways, big and small) – this was because some members of staff were illiterate and could not, therefore, read ordinary signs and notices. As noted in the text, part of the 1ft 11½in (nominal 2ft) gauge was retained for internal usage for a while after the closure of the Nantlle Tramway. We can also see 3ft 6in gauge lines and, on the farther section of the siding heading off to the right-hand side of the shed, there is a length of three-rail 'mixed gauge'. A modest quantity of dressed slates are stacked by the wall to await transportation. PHOTOGRAPH: C.H.A.TOWNLEY; COURTESY JIM PEDEN/I.R.S.

	BRITISH TRANSPORT COMMISSION	OUR REF.	LF8/32.
YOUR REF.	**BRITISH RAILWAYS**	DATE	23.10.62.
DATE			

TO   H. C. Johnson, Esq.,
General Manager,
EU   N.

FROM   LINE TRAFFIC MANAGER
LONDON MIDLAND REGION
MANCHESTER

...LETIN 71/7 Extn.

REVIEW OF CIRCUMSTANCES ON BRANCH LINES.
PENYGROES TO NANTLLE. (FREIGHT ONLY)

1. Description.

The Nantlle branch leaves the Caernarvon to Afon Wen line at Penygroes Station and consists of 1 mile 301 yds of single track worked by the 'one engine in steam' system. Nantlle station which is an unstaffed Full load and Coal Depot is the only station on the branch and is situated in the village of Talysarn (population approx. 1,500). The village of Nantlle (350 inhabitants) is 2 miles from the Station. Slate quarrying is the main trade of the area and this has fallen off considerably leading to a decline in the population of Nantlle in recent years.

Beyond Nantlle Goods Yard a 3' 6" gauge tramway runs in an easterly direction to the Pen-yr-Orsedd Slate Quarry. This line is owned by the B.T.C. but is worked by a privately owned tractor (the property of Pen-yr-Orsedd Quarry) and the freehold of the land on which the tramway is constructed is not owned by the Commission. Although the line has been maintained, at least in part, by the Commission there is no legal obligation on the Commission to keep the tramway open. It is thought possible that the Quarry owners may wish to take over our obligations with regard to the tramway in order to continue their use of this facility.

2. Traffic Receipts

		Merchandise & Mineral Traffic			Coal	
		Consignments.	Tons.	Receipts	Tons	Receipts
Forwarded	1960	112	821	£1,973	–	–
	1961	90	690	£1,837	30/	–
Received	1960	–	–	–	3002*	£5,780
	1961	1	6	–	1784	£3,241

Merchandise "Smalls" are delivered by Caernarvon Goods Motor.

* includes 1,106½t received for Wales Gas Board – now changed over to Methane Gas supplied by Grid.

/ two wagons of coal refused by consignee and reconsigned by senders.

3. Proposal

Closure of Nantlle Depot to all traffic, recovery of the track from Penygroes to Nantlle, and the termination of our commitments so far as the tramway from Nantlle to Pan-yr-Orsedd Quarry is concerned.

4. Estimated loss of receipts and extra costs

Merchandise, mineral traffic – Minerals ex Pen-yr-Orsedd Quarry		£796
Loss in receipts from coal traffic diverted to Penygroes		£ 32
		£828

5. Annual reduction in expenditure

District Engineer day to day maintenance	£1,800
Train movement costs	122*
Tramway maintenance	256

(No expenditure by D.E. on renewal expected over the next 5 years) £2,178

* 1959 figure.

Net annual saving by closure
£1,350 p.a.

7. Alternative facilities for freight traffic

Traffic	Label to	Full loads invoice to
Less than truck loads	Caernarvon (as now)	–
Full loads requiring cartage	Panygroes	Panygroes
Full loads S. to S.	as consigned	
Livestock	as consigned	
Coal, Coke and Patent Fuel	as consigned.	

Slate traffic forwarded by Dorothea Quarry is brought into Nantlle Station by road and although an additional 1½ miles cartage in each direction would be involved in forwarding the traffic from Panygroes it is anticipated that traffic would be retained to rail.

Pen-yr-Orsedd Slate Quarry use the tramway to work trucks to Nantlle and although the management appreciate the reasons for closure it is possible some of this traffic may be lost to rail.

Coal traffic is received by two merchants who rent stacking ground at Nantlle and both appreciate the position and have no objection transferring their business to Panygroes Station on condition they can retain their stacking ground at Nantlle.

FOR M. G. T. LAMBERT

tramway between Nantlle station and the quarries, by the end of the 1950s only one trip was required each week. In 1961 Dorothea Quarry – one of the two remaining quarries in the Vale of Nantlle – ceased using the tramway and subsequently dispatched its slate by road direct from the quarry. This meant that the tramway's only remaining customer was Pen-yr-Orsedd Quarry; it was considered that the upkeep of horses for just one quarry was not economical, and so the haulage was given over to a privately-owned farm tractor.

This situation prevailed only until 1963. The previous year, British Railways had looked closely at the Nantlle branch and, not altogether surprisingly, had proposed that the branch be closed and the track lifted. As will be seen from the accompanying report, BR realised that it actually had no legal obligation to maintain the 3ft 6in tramway beyond Nantlle station, and so the isolation of the tramway caused the authorities little concern.

The closure of the Nantlle branch was effected on Monday 2 December 1963. Latterly, the WTTs had still listed three freight trips per week. The lifting of the branch was undertaken between November 1965 and February 1966; interestingly, the BR document giving details of material recovered from the branch mentions one bracket signal (this was at Pen-y-Groes), two straight post signals (these were distant signals for the level crossing) and three 2-lever ground frames (at Nantlle station).

As for the 3ft 6in gauge tramway, it is thought that the last load of slate from the quarries passed over it in November 1963. Although the tramway became isolated as a result of the closure of the Pen-y-Groes–Nantlle branch, some sections of it continued to be used for the internal movement of wagons. That, however, did not last for very long, as the last sections of the tramway were lifted during 1968.

Railtour by horse – it is 5 May 1957, and many of the participants are clad in gabardine macs which were, of course, well nigh compulsory railtour-wear at the time. The macs might prompt a nostalgic smile nowadays but, forty-odd years on from now, what will be the general reaction to today's brightly coloured, slogan-bearing anoraks? Here, the train has just left Nantlle station yard. The wagons bear the symbol of Pen-yr-Orsedd Quarry. Note that there are two types of wagons – the first second and fourth wagons are of the 1-44 series and have wooden frames and sheet iron sides, while the third wagon has vertical struts. On both types, the wooden frames project beyond the body. Note the double-flanged wheels and the 'twin' check rails. We suspect that the horses are Mr.Oswald Jones's PRINCE and CORWEN. PHOTOGRAPH: DOUGLAS ROBINSON

Although that was the very end for the Nantlle branch and the old Nantlle tramway, the tradition of quarrying continued, albeit on a rather modest scale. Dorothea Quarry – once the largest and most profitable quarry in the Vale of Nantlle – lasted only until 1970, but Pen-yr-Orsedd Quarry continued on a small scale (i.e. with just 12 employees) until 1984. Interestingly, the internal 2ft gauge system at Pen-yr-Orsedd had been locomotive worked until the late autumn of 1970, when road tractors had taken over. Latterly, the quarry locomotives had been a quartet of Ruston & Hornsby 20hp four-wheeled diesels; two of the four had been there since 1945.

Contributors' note: *Some of the material for this article was gleaned from official railway company and Board of Trade files which were sourced at the Public Record Office, Kew. Other material came from contemporary railway magazines and from* Industrial Locomotives of North Wales *by V.J.Bradley (IRS, 1992). Also consulted was Volume One of J.I.C.Boyd's trilogy* Narrow Gauge Railways in North Caernarvonshire *– this is, without any question whatsoever, the definitive work.*

Railtour by tractor – it is now 20 October 1963 and, noted in the text, hor haulage has been repla by tractor haulage. not absolut precise here, b pect proach Quarry, lle Road o r the railto anised joint phenson Loco iety and the Ma Locomotive Society. A special train (locomotive worked!) started from Manchester Exchange at 9.35am and arrived at Bangor at about 1pm. Detours were made to the Bethesda, Llanberis and Nantlle branches, and the return trip set out from Bangor at 6.50pm, arriving back in Manchester at 9.45pm. The cost for this excellent day out was 37/6d from Manchester. PHOTOGRAPH: LYNDON W.ROWE

Engine sheds – but not as we know them, Jim...
Photographs by W.J.Ford

...Y BYLINES we occasionally ... which Aidan Fuller ...an Fuller was, of ...er of the fabled ...the famous little ha ... gave directions to ever ... ed in the land. The 'ones ... the engine sheds on indu... y systems. That said, it is v... us to imply that Flt-Lt Fulle... ly forgot those sheds – he was, ... t, heavily involved with the industrial railway scene and so he would have been perfectly well aware of all manner of industrial sheds up and down the country. It was no doubt a conscious decision of his *not* to attempt to list them in a handbook. After all, given that virtually every industrial railway in the land would have had some form of stabling and servicing facilities for its locomotives, there must have been well over a thousand industrial engine sheds in Britain. The production of a book covering all those sheds would have been a truly massive undertaking; to make the job even more difficult, many of the sheds were tucked away in obscure locations and were sparsely documented. Furthermore, it would have been more than a full-time job to ensure the information remained current – industrial railway systems could undergo fairly substantial changes without any outsiders being aware of it. But if an 'Industrial Locoshed Directory' had ever been published, it would have been absolutely fascinating, not least of all for the variety of engine sheds that was to be found. This pair of pictures provides a small sample of the variety that was on offer.

The upper picture shows a typical industrial shed scene – a somewhat ramshackle shed building (the wiggly tin structure in the mid-distance), 'minimalist' watering and coaling facilities, an abandoned Manning Wardle saddle tank, and the random scattering of discarded materials. This particular shed was on the Pitsford Quarries system in Northamptonshire; in the mid-distance on the left, the mineral wagons are standing on the exchange sidings alongside the Market Harborough-Northampton line (¼-mile or so to the south of Pitsford & Brampton station).

The lower picture shows the other end of the industrial scale. Pen Green engine shed (also known as Gretton Brook) was on the Corby Quarries system; it opened in August 1954 to replace several older sheds, and boasted roller doors, inspection pits, an overhead crane and strip lighting throughout. It could accommodate no less than forty locomotives on its eight roads. This shed was one of the very largest – and certainly one of the best equipped – engine sheds on any industrial system in the country. In fact, it put many BR engine sheds to shame.

Now, if Aidan Fuller *had* produced an 'Industrial Locoshed Directory', what are the chances that some of the directions would have included: "Turn left along a cinder path"? There *always* seemed to be a cinder path!

COVENTRY
HOMEFIRE PLANT
Nº 2

INCIDENT AT WHEELWRIGHT LANE
By Don Townsley; photographs by the author or from his collection

January 27th 1967 looked like being a typical Friday afternoon. I had just returned to the Hunslet works from a trip to Appleby Frodingham Steel Company at Scunthorpe and was checking through the post and messages to see if there was anything that would not wait until Monday. These were the days before mass car ownership, and to ease the burden on public transport the works and office finishing times were spaced thirty minutes apart. The last of the shop floor workers had departed their various ways and the Sergeant Commissionaire had commenced his daily round checking doors, windows and punch-clocks, whilst the Clerk of Works made the customary pre-weekend survey of power supplies and other critical items. The dreaded word 'security' with all its high-tech and obstructive implications was yet to impinge on the peace and orderliness of the manufacturing scene.

As I watched the steady trickle of homeward bound office workers passing my window the telephone rang. Experience had taught me that if you wanted a quiet weekend it was quite a good idea to avoid being anywhere near a telephone after three o'clock on a Friday afternoon, but an instinct for professional survival had taught me that the chance of a 'phone call offering the prospect of an order for a locomotive or locomotives was also at its highest after this time. It was a little bit like Russian Roulette – you eventually went home either rejoicing or lamenting. At least it was better than worrying all weekend about what you might have missed.

In the event, I answered the 'phone. "We have had a slight mishap with one of your locomotives", said the caller. "Can you send a service engineer down to advise on whether or not it can be put right on site?" It is a funny thing, but customers always referred to 'our' locomotive when everything was running smoothly but emphasised that it was 'your' locomotive when things went wrong.

No-one from the works staff would have answered an internal telephone call at that late hour, and so it was off across the yard to the Service Department to see if any unsuspecting service engineer was belatedly completing his weekly report and expense forms. Luck was on my side, and thus Dave Walker duly volunteered for an early Saturday morning trip to the Coventry Homefire smokeless fuel plant from whence the call had come. The proverbial buck having been successfully passed, I took my leave of the by now strangely quiet establishment.

The National Coal Board's Coventry Homefire Plant had been opened late in 1965 for the express purpose of manufacturing a flat multi-faceted smokeless fuel 'tablet' rather like a huge black three-penny bit. The formulation and shape of this product had been the brainchild of Dr.Bronowski, and much midnight oil had been burned in the design and development of the moulds and presses before satisfactory production could commence. This is an intriguing story in itself, but the provision of locomotives to handle the incoming raw materials and outgoing fin-

Above. COVENTRY HOMEFIRE PLANT No.2, Hunslet Engine Co W/No.6658 of 1965, poses for the camera shortly before delivery in early February 1966. The first locomotive, W/No.6657, had been despatched from the works to Coventry on 30 December 1965. The two-tone mid- and light Brunswick green livery with vermilion dividing bands shows up to good effect. Black and yellow chevrons were the norm by this time for buffer beams; handrails were grey and the radiator mesh and nameplate backgrounds were picked out in vermilion. The fuel tank projections on to the footplates were black, as were the frames, stair wells and buffer face plates.

Left. W/No.6658 marshals a train of coal in the outwards sidings of Coventry Colliery early in 1966 – the Homefire plant is taking shape in the background mist. The locomotive will then proceed to the other end of the train to depart stage left towards the British Rail exchange sidings. The 16-ton mineral wagons with plain axle bearings and hand brakes only were still the mainstay of the National Coal Board's operations at this time.

Having marshalled its train, W/No.6658 has now run round to the 'country' end and, with the brakes pinned down on every fourth wagon, is ready to proceed to the exchange sidings at Lythalls Lane. The end of the train is hidden by the row of wooden internal user wagons at the far right of the picture, but the load appears to be at least twenty-two full wagons – this would be in excess of 450 tons. The train is on the colliery exit line; the equivalent line for the Homefire Plant can be seen by the fence at extreme left.

Not what we expected... Three views of the then recently laid entrance road into the Homefire Plant reception sidings give some idea as to why relationships between different departments were sometimes a little cool. These pictures were taken before the plant reached any measurable level of production, but the track has already moved by some twelve inches from where it should have been.

ished product was only marginally less difficult.

The Plant was built at Keresley alongside Coventry Colliery at the extremity of a 1¾-mile branch from a point just north of Three Spires Junction near Foleshill on the former L&NWR Coventry-Nuneaton line. The branch left the L&NWR line in a facing direction approaching from Coventry just beyond the Lythalls Lane bridge and, turning left, fanned out into Lythalls Lane exchange sidings. After turning further left through almost ninety degrees, it then almost immediately started to climb at a ruling gradient of 1 in 49 up to the plateau on which was situated Coventry Colliery. The colliery was on the right hand side of the line at the top of the incline; falling ground on the left hand side was gradually made up to accommodate the smokeless fuel plant, as it developed, together with another large fan of sidings. The stability of this siding land was for long a bone of contention as the track was prone to shifting sideways under the weight of the incoming loaded coal trains and outgoing smokeless fuel.

Prior to the coming of the smokeless fuel plant the branch had been single track. With the addition of another track on the left-hand, or western, side it now gave the impression of being double track but in reality was worked as two independent single lines. The left-hand line carried traffic both ways for the smokeless fuel plant whilst the right hand track similarly served Coventry Colliery. The former was

Not what we expected – take two.

Not what we expected – take three.

thus under the jurisdiction of NCB Coal Products Division from their offices in Lyon Road, Harrow, whilst the latter was controlled from NCB East Midlands Division No.7 Area at Cole Orton Hall, Ashby-de-la-Zouch. As the Coventry coal was not of the quality required for conversion into smokeless fuel it was therefore possible, after the plant went into production, to see loaded coal trains travelling up grade on the left hand track and down grade on the right hand track, thereby emphasising the double track illusion. However, this illusion was dispelled by the spectacle of loaded smokeless fuel trains coming down on the left-hand side while empty wagons went up to the colliery on the right-hand side.

To add to the operating interest there was an extremely busy level crossing serving Wheelwright Lane at around the midpoint of the gradient. This crossing was protected by gates which were permanently manned during operational hours. In addition, catch points before the crossing on each of the two lines in a downgrade direction led into substantial sand drags to guard against run-aways. Wheelwright Lane provided direct road access into the Coventry city centre and to the large factories of Courtaulds, Daimler and Dunlop.

For the opening of the plant, Coal Products Division had ordered two 60ton 0-8-0 diesel locomotives from the Hunslet Engine Company Limited. Each locomotive had two Cummins NT400 diesel engines, and the resulting 776hp made them the most powerful industrial diesel-hydraulic locomotives at that time in the country. Mechanically, they were effectively two of Hunslet's standard 0-6-0 locomotives mounted back to back on an eight-wheeled rigid frame and sharing a common cab. Carrying Works Nos. 6657 and 6658 and with cast brass plates on the cab side

COVENTRY HOMEFIRE PLANT No.1 and COVENTRY HOMEFIRE PLANT No.2 they were despatched on 30 December 1965 and 8 February 1966 respectively. The livery was the makers standard of two tone mid- and light Brunswick green. The mid-green was on the valances and on the upper and lower extremities of the superstructure, with a broad central band of light green between. The two shades were separated by two-inch wide bands of vermilion running along the line of the engine casing hinges.

During 1965 the Homefire plant was in its final stages of construction and the trackwork was being completed. While the diesel locomotives were under construction, Hunslet loaned two 'Austerity' 0-6-0STs to undertake the trial runs and generally help out with construction. These locomotives were from a mixed bag of fifteen, which had been re-purchased by Hunslet as surplus from the Army over a period from 1960. They were slowly being rebuilt, mostly with underfeed stokers, and re-sold to collieries up and down the country. The first to go to Coventry was W/No.3163 of 1944 (re-built as W/No. 3885 of 1963) on the first of May 1965. A rather hurried entry into the exchange sidings one day resulted in a bruising encounter with a British Railways Brush type 2 Bo-Bo Diesel Electric, and neither of the two antagonists were ever quite the same again. As a result, Bagnall Austerity, W/No.2774 of 1945 was also sent to the plant in September 1965. This locomotive had been allocated rebuilt Hunslet Works No.3893, but had only received a light repair and, although earmarked for fitting with an underfeed stoker, did not actually acquire one before going to Coventry.

Both of the loaned Austerity 0-6-0STs were returned to Hunslet on 24 May 1966. The company's order book was pretty full

at the time and so there was no hurry to do any work on them. The slightly misshapen W/No.3885 was later sold (in 1969) to NCB Western Area in 'as-is' condition and was repaired at Walkden Workshops. It subsequently went to Gresford Colliery where it was named ALISON and later to Bold Colliery where it was renamed JOSEPH. It finished up at the Chatterley Whitfield Mining Museum near Stoke-on-Trent. In January 1988 the Museum sent W/No.3885 to Crewe Heritage Centre for 'restoration' from where it returned on 6 December 1991. The already much-travelled W/No.3885 moved in April 1992 to the Swanage Railway; it later went to the South Devon Railway.

Going back to the time of W/No.3885's disposal by Hunslet to the NCB Western Area in 1969, the political climate which, on the one hand, was endorsing the Clean Air Act and generally outlawing steam locomotive pollution (hence the allegedly pollution-free underfeed stoker) and, on the other, trying to placate miners at the deep mine collieries who were reluctant to accept diesel locomotives, was beginning to cool. Consequently, when the Bagnall Austerity returned from the Coventry Homefire Plant to Hunslet Engine Co, there was no purchaser for it. It was cut up at the works during 1969. To all intents and purposes industrial steam in Britain had been put on final notice. W/No. 3885's reprieve had been a one-off flash in the pan.

But what of the incident, which prompted this article in the first place? While we at Hunslet valued every customer – it was they who paid our wages, after all – the Coventry Homefire was regarded from the start as the 'customer from hell'. It was not the operators' fault that the plant was in the wrong place at the top of a steep hill. It was not their fault either that the close proximity of

the then all-powerful motor car works had first pick of skilled engineers and maintenance men. Nor could they be blamed for the fact that, for quite a long time, the smokeless fuel briquettes, instead of coming easily out of the moulds in which they were produced, stuck in vast quantities. These problems were an almost inevitable consequence of developing the plant on that particular site, but that was of little consolation to the people who had to look after the day-to-day running of the plant. Morale at the plant was often low, suitably qualified personnel were difficult to find, let alone keep, and generally the whole operation of the railway left quite a lot to be desired.

Immediately after leaving the 'fulls outwards' sidings, a departing train was on the relentless, almost dead-straight, 1 in 49 descent, and any runaway had little chance of completing its journey in one piece. Suitable hopper wagons with continuous brakes, either vacuum or air, were years away and the rule at the plant was for a number of wagons, usually at least one in four, to have their brakes pinned down in the time-honoured fashion of the steam era. Furthermore, it was stipulated that the locomotive should wait at the top of the incline and not proceed until the brakes had been pinned. On 27 January 1967 the rules appear not to have been obeyed, and one of our diesels, COVENTRY HOMEFIRE PLANT No.1, and its train came to grief. Reports of the incident were varied, but one suggested that the train came on to the gradient at a speed of around 9mph, indicating that no stop had been made to pin down brakes, and from then on a pile-up of some magnitude was inevitable.

Fortunately, the crossing keeper at Wheelwright Lane seemed to have noticed that something was amiss. With the crossing gates already closed to road traffic, he set the points into the long sand drag on the top side of the crossing, alerted what emergency services were appropriate, (not a lot in 1967!), and waited. The wait was not a long one. The 60-ton locomotive hauling (or, more correctly, being pushed by) what the *Coventry Evening Telegraph* described as '21 trucks carrying about 400 tons of coal' careered through the catch points and associated sand drag to settle down almost at the foot of gardens in Houldsworth Crescent.

Mercifully, there were no reports of any injuries. The 35-year-old driver and his 18-year-old assistant had vacated their places of work prior to the cavalcade coming to rest, which was just as well. With the locomotive frame buried almost to rail-level the leading wagon ran along the footplate, taking the trailing diesel power unit with it, it came to rest at thirty degrees to the horizontal atop the by-now-demolished driving cab. Apart from the superstructure damage to the locomotive and the need for a new power unit everything else was in remarkably good order, but it was not the sort of repair job which David Walker could put right on site.

The reference in the *Coventry Evening Telegraph* to the load being 400 tons of coal is an interesting point. The Homefire Plant for which the locomotives had been purchased, and on which the then enormous sum of £12 million had been spent, was scheduled to produce 4,250 tons of smokeless fuel per week on opening in early 1966. It didn't. As late as 27 November 1967 – i.e. eleven months after the accident – the 'Telegraph' was reporting that a maximum output of only 700 tons per week was being achieved, and even that meagre amount was intermittent, between plant breakdowns.

At the time of this feverish inactivity the locomotive fleet of Coventry Colliery, across the way, comprised the three ex-BR outside-cylinder pannier tanks, Nos.1501, 1502 and 1509. The local residents objected strongly to the smoke nuisance from these steam locomotives and for most of the time from 1965 until 1969 the Homefire diesels did most of the colliery work – this was in addition to their own duties. By 1969 enough smokeless fuel was being ejected from the moulds to provide a reasonable work load for the two eight-wheeled diesels, and I must confess to then selling two 534hp six-wheeled diesels to the colliery, thereby sealing the fate of the panniers. Fortunately, though, one of them, No.1501, escaped into preservation.

The newspaper reference to the train conveying coal, plus photographs of the incident, confirm that the leading wagons did contain coal and not smokeless fuel. This suggests that the train was on a colliery trip. In this case it should have been on the right hand road, not the left, looking up to the colliery. My memory of those days does not recall a connection between the colliery and Homefire Plant tracks to the upside of Wheelwright Lane crossing, so how coal came to be travelling 'wrong road' will probably remain one of life's little mysteries. Unless, of course, the leading wagons were carrying surplus or rejected coal for some reason.

From David Walker's report an assessment was made of the cost of repair work necessary to return the unfortunate COVENTRY HOMEFIRE PLANT No.1 to full working order. Eventually, authorisation to proceed with the re-habilitation was given and the locomotive, suitably sheeted over, was conveyed by road to the Hunslet works from where it was returned in September 1967 looking to all intents

No, we would rather not try to put this right on site... COVENTRY HOMEFIRE PLANT No.1 rests somewhat inelegantly, having run through the sand drag. The trailing radiator lies under the drawgear of the leading wagon, while the engine is hidden under the mangled remains of the cab. The rear portion of the train stands on the 'main' line, either having been drawn back after the incident or uncoupled before the impact.

and purposes like a new machine.

Despite the severity of the impact, there was virtually no damage other than that which had been immediately apparent. As a natural precaution the locomotive was stripped down to the basic frame so that frame alignment could be checked and the horn-gaps measured to ensure that correct axlebox clearances were maintained. It came as no surprise that the riveted structure with its 3ft deep by 3ins thick frame-plates, 4ins thick buffer beams and robust welded stretchers had not flinched and there was no evidence of twist or bending. The locomotive had been designed to provide the maximum adhesive weight possible within the railway's infrastructure restraints, and Hunslet's policy of building this weight into the frame structure instead of using cast iron or coagulated metal punchings as ballast was vindicated.

It was, however, necessary to provide a new diesel engine and hydraulic transmission for the trailing (No.2) end of the locomotive, together with the attendant radiator and engine casing assembly. The driving cab was straightened and fitted with new windows and, after careful reassembly and repainting of the locomotive, there was nothing to show for what could have been quite a serious incident, had the sand drag not been provided as a precaution.

It would be difficult even for me in my biased position, having sold the locomotives in the first place, to claim that they were trouble-free in service. They survived until 1984, but from 1980 had been largely superseded by a series of British Rail Class 08 350hp diesel-electric shunters hired locally from BR. The 08s handled shorter trains, but more of them, and in any case the plant output never reached the original planned figure. One of the idiosyncratic aspects of industrial railways was that locomotives would quite often be loaded up to the limit of their capabilities, even if that meant running only one train per day. In this respect the Homefire Plant ran true to form and, by 1980, fifteen years of slogging up, and braking on the way down, the long 1 in 49 gradient had taken their toll. From the outset, the limited resources had made it difficult to maintain the locomotives to ensure that the twin engines and gearboxes worked in unison. This lack of maintenance had inevitably added to the wear and tear.

In 1982 Grant Lyon Eagre Construction Ltd partly relaid the colliery sidings and approach track, and the installation of a rapid-loading bunker allowed the colliery to switch over to air braked MGR wagons by 1983. MGR wagons also came into use on the Homefire Plant traffic and thus came about the requirement for the plant's own locomotives to have BR-compatible twin-pipe air-braking equipment. This introduction of continuous braking removed the basic cause of the 1967 runaway – namely a lack of sufficient and sure braking capacity – and the roller bearing fitted wagons considerably reduced the power required for traction. But it was all somewhat late in the day.

Three of the four Hunslet 0-6-0 diesels at the colliery (two more had been transferred there, one in 1977 and the other in 1979) were converted to provide air train braking, and in 1989 two of the large 75-ton GEC diesel-electrics were drafted in from the then shrinking Staffordshire coalfield. The poor state of the Homefire eight-wheelers dispelled all thoughts of train brake conversions, and both eight-wheelers were scrapped on site by Atherstone Iron & Steel Co Ltd in October 1984. They were replaced by a pair of ex-Port of Bristol Authority 0-6-0 Sentinel diesel-hydraulics. These were supplied by Thomas Hill (Rotherham) Ltd who had rebuilt them with train air brakes and arranged for them to operate as a tandem pair. A third Rolls Royce Sentinel locomotive, which had previously been at Birch Coppice Colliery, provided a standby unit.

It is some years now since I had reason to visit the Homefire site, and I must thank Bob Darvill of the Industrial Railway Society for help in providing an update with which to close off this account. In late 1995 the Doncaster firm of Trackwork Limited were working on the branch to upgrade the infrastructure for main-line working and to install automatic crossing gates. Some trains worked over the line after this work was done, but the new equipment actually saw very little use. Coventry Colliery closed in August 1996 and it is doubtful if there were any workings after that date. There were a number of items in the press stating that a new industrial estate was to be built on the site of the colliery and that the line was being retained for that purpose but, so far, these schemes seem to have come to naught.

The Homefire Plant Sentinel and Rolls Royce locomotives were reported as working in February 1993, but by July 1994 all the locomotives were out of use. The three that remained were all sold to Staffordshire Locomotives in January 1996.

The crew were lucky to be able to escape through the cab rear doors before the impact. Surprisingly, the leading wagons load of coal appears to be intact.

COVENTRY
HOMEFIRE PLANT
Nº 1

The diesel engine should be where the wagon wheels are, but is presumably hidden amongst the mass of metal which had been forced into the cab. Foam has been sprayed on the oil spillage from the fuel tank, the tank having been displaced from its position on the running plate.

PANNIERS BESIDE LOCH FLEET
A brief history of the Dornoch Light Railway.

'...No.15053 works the Dornoch Light Railway; it was observed, neatly shedded, in the evening, and on the 9.10am train the next morning. According to the engine crew, this little machine has its boiler washed out once a fortnight, and goes to Inverness about every four months'.

The attractive seaside town of Dornoch, the county town of Sutherland in the north of Scotland, is famed for its tiny cathedral and impressive golf courses, and is effortlessly reached by the A9 road which crosses the Dornoch Firth and enters the town from the south. The town is some six miles from the nearest railway, the former Highland Railway Inverness-Wick main line though, at one time, there was a branch which left the main line at The Mound and entered Dornoch from the north.

Unfortunately, this stretch of main line is where the Highland had to make a major diversion inland to Lairg, followed by nearly twenty miles of unremunerative line before Golspie was reached. It might seem more logical for Dornoch's railway to have branched from the main line somewhere around Tain and to have struck northwards across the Dornoch Firth – not noted for its maritime traffic – thereby cutting thirty-six miles or so from the journey between Dornoch and Inverness. However, the problem with such a line would have been the crossing of the Dornoch Firth – as the firth was 1½ miles wide, a railway bridge would have been extremely costly, probably prohibitively so. Thus, Dornoch's rail connection between the years 1902 and

by
A.J. Mullay and I.C.Coleford

1960 took the form of a branch line from The Mound; to outward appearances this was a fairly conventional branch line but, legally, it was a *light* railway. The Light Railways Act of 1896 was intended to aid and simplify the construction of lines to remote areas, and Treasury grants were available to lines which, in the opinion of the Board of Agriculture or Board of Trade, would '...benefit agriculture in any district' or where '...a necessary means of communication would be established between a fishing harbour or fishing village and a market, or that such a railway is necessary for the development of or maintenance of some definite industry'. The Act was well-intentioned, but it was open to exploitation and there were many instances of 'main line' companies setting up nominal subsidiaries for the promotion and construction of light railways with, of course, the aid of Government grants. In the case of the Dornoch Light Railway, the company *was* completely independent although, as we shall see later, it had a close corporate relationship with the Highland Railway.

The Dornoch Light Railway Company was formed in 1898 to take advantage of the Act, and the venue of its first recorded board meeting – the office of the Sutherland estates – shows that the local aristocrat, the Duke of Sutherland, was very supportive of the venture. He took no fewer than 5,000 shares in the company, many times more than either Dornoch Town Council or Sutherland County Council. All felt that the town, irrespective of its modest population of around 1,000, should have a rail connection, as befitted a county capital.

Capitalised at £22,000, the Dornoch Light Railway (DLR) obtained its Light Railway Order on 13 August 1898, authorising the construction of a 7¾-mile line from the Highland Railway's Far North main-line at The Mound, with which Dornoch was then connected by a mail gig service. (The Mound itself is a 1,000-yard-long embankment – intended partly for use as a road and partly to reclaim some land for agricultural use – which had been engineered by Thomas

As related later in the text, in July 1955 No.55053 was treated to a very smart fully lined livery during its repair at St.Rollox Works. This proved to be rather fitting, as the engine soon claimed the distinction of being the very last ex-Highland locomotive in ordinary BR service. It was photographed at Dornoch on 10 August 1956. Note the ground frame at the neck of the station yard. PHOTOGRAPH: N.SWIFT; THE TRANSPORT TREASURY

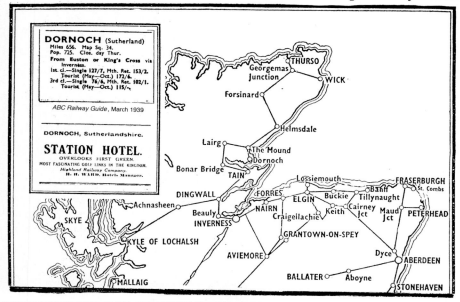

One of the two surviving ex-Highland Railway 0-4-4Ts, No.55051, waits at the branch platform at The Mound on 27 May 1949. Although the locomotive has received its post-Nationalisation lettering and a smokebox number-plate, the days of smokebox shed plates are still a year or so into the future. The coach, which is lettered 'LMS', is one of the 'Diagram 1755' 57ft vehicles which had been built at Wolverton in 1926/27; attached to the rear is an ex-Southern Railway parcels van. Note the water tower at the far end of the branch platform. The main line platform of the Inverness-Wick line is on a slightly higher level behind. A train stands at the up main platform; note the use of the singular 'platform' – there was only one main line platform at The Mound. Although there was a passing loop, this was only for goods trains – it was not authorised for passenger trains. PHOTOGRAPH: J.W.ARMSTRONG TRUST

Telford and completed in 1817). The Order specified that the rails needed to be only 56lbs per yard, and no 'shelters or conveniences' needed to be constructed at any of three intermediate stations, at Cambusavie*, Skelbo, and Embo. Fares were not to exceed 3d per mile for first class passengers, 2d for second class, and 1d for third class. The light railway company's minute books for October 1901 refer to the possible construction of an additional passenger platform at Littleferry, but this came to naught. *(* The timetable for the day the line opened – 2 June 1902 –*

lists only Skelbo and Embo, but the timetable for the very next day also lists Cambusavie; one assumes that Cambusavie – with its minimalist facilities – was probably ready for 2 June, but no trains actually stopped there on that day). With a junction with the Highland's 'Far North' line at The Mound, it was always envisaged that the Highland Railway would work the line, and an unusual 25-year lease of locomotives and rolling-stock was negotiated by the infant company, one which had to be revised so that the DLR could pay off the £2,500 capital

sum and interest in annual payments, with depreciation being allowed for – this was something the Highland had failed to include. All operational staff were employed by the Highland, the Dornoch company's sole employee being the Secretary. But despite the strong Highland influence, the light railway company was to maintain its independence until Grouping in 1923.

A Treasury grant of £14,000 was received, but with the original contractor going bankrupt, the DLR had to request an additional £1,445 after opening; of that extra sum, £945 was received by December 1903. The cost of building the line was actually £30,000, with the Highland being asked to step in urgently in 1900 to secure a road bridge at The Mound, the contractor having left work unfinished. Most unusually for a light railway, the Board of Trade had insisted that the line should have fencing for its entire length and gates at all level crossings. The construction of five crossings – Dornoch Plantation, Embo, Skelbo Castle, Cambusavie and at the south end of The Mound – complete with crossing keeper's cottages, had been costed at £1,113.3.0d and had been authorised at a meeting of the light railway company's directors on 8 March 1901. The gates at each of the crossings, incidentally, were protected by hand-operated signals. The total cost of signalling and interlocking throughout the line was £1,039.14.11d.

At one time no fewer than 98 men were working on this short line on which the only major earthwork was the Fleet Via-

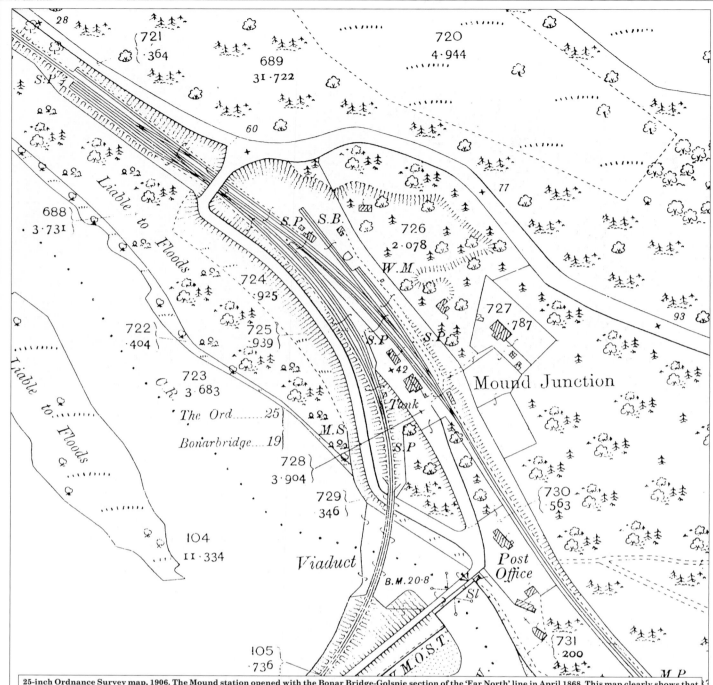

25-inch Ordnance Survey map, 1906. The Mound station opened with the Bonar Bridge-Golspie section of the 'Far North' line in April 1868. This map clearly shows that the station was in the middle of nowhere; it served only as a point of exchange for Dornoch – prior to the opening of the Dornoch branch in 1902 it had been the point where mail coaches to and from Dornoch had met the 'main line' trains, thus explaining the existence of a Post Office in such an isolated spot. Note that, although The Mound station had a passing loop, it had only one main line platform – the passing loop was authorised only for goods trains, and so passenger trains could not cross here. CROWN COPYRIGHT

duct, a steel girder structure with trough flooring, and having four arches each of 50 feet span; the principal gradient on the railway was the 1 in 45 from the north end of viaduct up to The Mound station. From the south end of the viaduct the line ran beside Loch Fleet – now a National Nature Reserve – before traversing an area of sand dunes, skirting the Royal Dornoch Golf Course and terminating within a stone's throw of Dornoch's 13th century cathedral. As per the original proposal, the three intermediate stations were Cambusavie (1¼ miles from The Mound), Skelbo (3¾ miles) and Embo (5½ miles).

The line opened to public passenger traffic on 2 June 1902. The engine in charge, not only on opening day, but also for the first three years of the line's existence, was Highland Railway 0-6-0T

No.56, formerly named BALNAIN, but renamed DORNOCH for its new sphere of duties. It was one of three similar locomotives which had been built at the Highland's Lochgorm Works in Inverness between 1869 and 1874. These little engines had a maximum axleweight of only 10 tons, which made them ideal for lightly-constructed lines such as the Dornoch branch. They were designed by William Stroudley who left the Highland Railway for the London, Brighton & South Coast Railway in 1870; within a few months of taking up his new post at Brighton, Stroudley made slight alterations to the design for a new type of tank engine for the LB&SCR. These were the famous 'Terriers' – the rest, as they say, is history.

During the first three months of operation, the Dornoch branch generated gross receipts of £561.19.9d, against

£379.19.5d in expenses. It carried nearly 45,000 people in its first year, rising to 47,419 in its second. Train mileage was 15,972 in the second year, with expenses per train mile stated to be "26.33" – this was presumably old pence. There were three trains each way daily in the first timetable, with an additional one on Tuesdays. Local historian Barry Turner has suggested that the extra train on that day was to serve those Sutherland citizens attending court in their county town, but one wonders if Sutherland was so full of miscreants as to justify such a service! The extra train was certainly not likely to have been intended to carry market traffic, as the Highland Railway timetable omitted Dornoch from the list of market towns it served.

By the following autumn, train times had changed slightly. Although the Tues-

The primitive-looking 4,000 gallon water tank was on the 'headshunt' of the engine shed at Dornoch. To the left of the tower, a wagon stands at the timber coal stage. The single-storey building beyond the stage is a storage hut for a private trader's coal. On the extreme right of the picture is the wall of the engine shed. The building cost £225.14.0d to construct. It has been suggested elsewhere that the shed was built on the site of the well-known local historical monument, St. Michael's Well, but that is not true... As explained in Bentinck's history of Dornoch, published in 1926, the well was actually sited just to the south of where the passenger station was built (its position is clearly marked on the accompanying Ordnance Survey map). However, in the early 1830s the parliamentary boundary of the burgh was defined, with St.Michael's Well being designated its north-easterly limit. The Act defining this boundary stipulated that owners of properties more than seven miles outside the boundary should have no vote in the burgh's affairs, but one prominent local citizen lived a hundred yards or so beyond the 'seven-mile limit' and was thereby deprived of his vote. This gentleman issued instructions for a stone structure bearing the inscription 'St. Michael's Well' to be erected some 200 yards north of the actual site (where the engine shed was to be built in 1902). Taking this marker as the boundary of Dornoch, the gentleman's residence came within the 'seven-mile limit' and he thereby retained his vote! Thus, the 'well' on the site of the engine shed was merely a marker, not the well itself. PHOTOGRAPH: P.J.GARLAND

day special had vanished altogether, there were now four trains each weekday – two passenger and two mixed. The 7½ miles between The Mound and Dornoch were covered in 25-30 minutes by the passenger trains, with the mixed trains taking an average of eight minutes longer. Cambusavie was a request stop throughout the life of the branch.

In 1902 the Highland Railway's Locomotive Superintendent, Peter Drummond, proposed the construction of new lightweight tank locomotives specifically for working, not only the Dornoch branch, but also the soon-to-be-opened Lybster branch which was also built to Light Railway specifications. Although the HR board initially agreed to the construction of two such locomotives, Drummond came up with two alternative proposals, the first for a petrol-engined railbus and the second for a steam railmotor. Neither of those alternatives was considered acceptable, and so thoughts reverted to small tank engines. Four were constructed between March 1905 and February 1906. They were smart little 0-4-4Ts with 4ft 6in driving wheels and a very modest maximum axleweight of 11¼ tons. Two of the quartet (HR Nos.45 and 46) were frequently used on the Dornoch branch, the other two (Nos.25 and 40) appearing less frequently; it seems that they initially shared the work with the Stroudley 0-6-0T, No.56, and occasionally (in later years, at least) Jones 0-4-4T No.53.

The branch engine was kept in a small timber-built shed at Dornoch. The shed was nominally an outstation of Inverness, but it seems that routine maintenance of the Dornoch branch engines was undertaken at Helmsdale, another of Inverness' sub-sheds. According to Cormack & Stevenson's ex-

WORKING OF BRANCH LINES.

The following Branch Lines are worked with Lock and Key, and not more than *one* Engine in steam must be allowed on the respective Sections or Branches at one and the same time, viz. :—

Wick and Lybster Light Railway.
Dornoch and The Mound Light Railway.
Muir of Ord and Fortrose (Black Isle Branch).
Gollanfield and Fort-George.
Orbliston and Fochabers Town

All connecting Points at Intermediate Stations, as well as those at Lybster, Dornoch, and Fort-George Terminals, are secured by a Lock, the Key of which is under the charge of the Engine Driver.

When Shunting has to be performed at any of these Stations, the Driver will hand the Key to the Stationmaster or Guard of the Train, who will relieve the Levers, and when operations have been completed, will again return it to the Driver, who must not proceed on his journey without its being in his possession.

No Engine must at any time enter upon the Main Line of these Branches until the Driver of such Engine has first received into his possession the Key in use on the Section.

When, under any circumstances, there is a change of Engine Drivers, the Stationmaster or person in charge at the Station where the change is made will accept of the Key from the one Driver and pass it to the other, giving and obtaining a written acknowledgment.

The Staff Key for Working Branch Lines must on completion of each day's work be handed over by Engine Driver to the Stationmaster or person in charge at Terminal Station.

The Key must be kept in a place of security over night, and handed to Engine Driver each morning before despatch of first Train.

Extract from the Highland Railway WTT Appendix for 1920.

The branch terminus at Dornoch was a modeller's delight – a single dead-end platform, a modest goods yard, and a small engine shed (unfortunately out of view here). On 30 July 1952 No.55051 is undertaking some shunting – goods wagons will be attached behind the carriage and parcels van, and the train will run 'mixed' to The Mound. The carriage, the first of a batch of twenty-five brake corridor composites which had been built for the LMSR in 1927, is numbered SC6659M and is in BR carmine and cream livery; photographer Tim Shuttleworth noted that the brass door hinges were stamped 'LNWR' – presumably, the North Western had kept a good stock of door hinges! The parcels van (an 8-ton meat van, in fact) is numbered M172609 and is painted brown. PHOTOGRAPH: F.W.SHUTTLEWORTH

DORNOCH BRANCH LIGHT RAILWAY

Skelbo Level Crossing.—After up trains have passed over the level crossing they must be brought to a stand and not proceed until the porter has opened the gates for the roadway and joined the train. Down trains must stop short of the level crossing to permit of the guard opening the gates for the passage of the train.

Left. Extract from the LMSR Northern Division WTT Appendix for 1937.

No.55051 positions the goods vans and wagons which it brought in from The Mound as part of a mixed train; the brake van on the left was part of the mixed train. The date is 30 July 1952. The Railway Clearing House *Handbook of Stations* stated that Dornoch station could deal with 'Goods, Passenger, Parcels and Miscellaneous Traffic, Furniture Vans, Carriages, Motor Cars, Portable Engines and Machines on Wheels, Livestock, Horse Boxes and Prize Cattle Vans, and Carriages and Motor Cars by Passenger or Parcels Train', and had a 30-cwt crane. Track plans of the late 1950s indicate that, whereas most of the station yard had, by then, been relaid with 75lb or 80lb rails, flat-bottomed rails were still *in situ* for most of the length of the goods shed road. PHOTOGRAPH: F.W.SHUTTLEWORTH

cellent *Highland Railway Locomotives* (RCTS, 1988), on one morning each week during the winter and three mornings during the summer, the branch train was advertised to run through to Brora and return, with the 0-4-4T or, occasionally, the old Stroudley 0-6-0T, working it throughout.

Apart from the introduction of the Drummond 0-4-4Ts in 1905, the short-lived working through to Brora, and the laying *circa* 1918 of a private timber siding near the Dornoch end of the line, little else changed on the branch over the years. Nevertheless, the light railway brought an unforeseen bonus to the town of Dornoch – this took the form of a luxury hotel which had been opened within two years of the railway's arrival. The hotel was appropriately named the Station

Hotel; after the demise of the railway it was renamed the Dornoch Hotel, and is still going strong, with visitors enjoying their golf by the North Sea. During World War I, incidentally, the hotel had been taken over for military use, first by the Gordon Highlanders and, later, by the Canadian Forestry Corps. As will be seen from the accompanying extracts from official documents, the line was worked on the 'one engine in steam' principle.

The line remained profitable until 1920, its first annual loss coming in 1921 when the deficit was £744.4.6d; fortuitously, the directors were able to cover this from a £800 reserve fund which had been prudently built up during the good years. The following year the loss increased to £826.18.0d.

LMSR days

The 1923 Grouping saw both the Dornoch Light Railway Company and the Highland Railway become part of the London Midland & Scottish Railway, but this had little effect on services. However, the Grouping brought about some change in the boardroom as, when the light railway company was wound up, the princely sum of £6.3.6d in unpaid dividends passed to the LMSR which, in turn, paid £350 towards winding-up costs. As the Company Secretary was the only employee by then, and was about to be made redundant, £300 of this was paid to him. More serious, however, was the loss of local control, for the light railway company's board minutes show a high level of management expertise, and above all, of concern for the well-being of the line. That could never be replicated by the LMSR which proved to be a highly-centralised company with its head office 656¼ (!) rail miles away at Euston.

At the time of the Grouping, the branch was served by three passenger trains each way on weekdays:
From Dornoch: 10.55am; 1.05pm; 4.40pm
From The Mound: 11.40am; 2.00pm; 6.43pm

These services were timed to connect with main line trains at The Mound – they were not aimed at purley local travellers as there was not really anywhere 'purley local' to go. The connections were:
• The 10.55am ex-Dornoch and 11.40am ex-The Mound connected with the 8.00am Wick-Inverness
• The 1.05pm ex-Dornoch and 2.00pm ex-The Mound connected with the 10.30am Inverness-Wick
• The 4.40pm ex-Dornoch connected with the 2.00pm Wick-Inverness
• The 6.43pm ex-The Mound connected with the 2.35pm Inverness-Helmsdale.

The locomotives most closely connected with the Dornoch branch duly received LMSR numbers:
• Drummond 0-4-4T No.20, 40, 45 and 46 became LMSR No.15051, 15052, 15053 and 15054 respectively.
• Stroudley 0-6-0T No.56 became LMSR No.16118 (by the mid-1920s, this engine was no longer seen on the Dornoch branch).
• Jones 0-4-4T No.53A (its duplicate number had been applied in 1917), became LMSR No.15050.

By the mid-1920s the veteran No.16118 was no longer seen on the Dornoch branch (it was withdrawn in 1928), and Jones 0-4-4T No.15050 was withdrawn in December 1929. By the early 1930s the usual pairing on the

This is a reduction from the 25-inch Ordnance Survey map of 1905. The little station nestles on the north side of the small town. The building at the north end of the station on the east of the line is the engine shed. The station layout seems to have been little altered throughout its 58-year working life. Note the Station Hotel in its own grounds on the east of the town. The 'Site of St.Michael's Well' is marked – the, shall we say, historical inaccuracy of this 'site' has been referred to in one of our earlier photo captions, but it seems that the Dornoch Light Railway Company knew not of the inaccuracy – the company minutes for October 1901 noted that a platform (within the shed) should be 're-erected' (this suggests an existing structure being dismantled and transferred to the Dornoch line) '...as near to the ancient site as possible... the site to be such that the edifice will not interfere with the laying of rails'. CROWN COPYRIGHT

	DORNOCH AND THE MOUND															
		1	2	3	4	5			1	2	3	4	5			
Miles	**WEEK DAYS**	MIXED		PASSENGER		Calls when required.	Miles	**WEEK DAYS**	MIXED		MIXED		Calls when required.			
		a.m.		p.m.					a.m.		p.m.					
0	DORNOCH .. ◊ ..dep.	10 40	..	1 10	..	**A**	0	THE MOUND .. ◊ ..dep.	11 50	..	2 0	..	**A**			
2¼	Embo	10 47	....	1 17	....		1¼	Cambusavie Platform	**A**	....	**A**	....				
4	Skelbo	10 59	....	1 24	....		3½	Skelbo	12 3	....	2 13	....				
6½	Cambusavie Platform	**A**	....	**A**	....		5½	Embo	12 9	....	2 19	....				
7¾	THE MOUND .. ◊ ..arr.	11 11	..	1 37	..		7¾	DORNOCH .. ◊ ..arr.	12 18	..	2 28	..				

LMSR working timetable, Summer 1947.

No.15052 had been withdrawn as long ago as December 1930, while No.15054 had been retired in October 1945.

However, it had long since become clear that the arrival of the railway some forty years earlier had not arrested the depopulation of the area. The population of the entire parish, according to the 1891 census, had been 2,404, but by the late 1930s it had dropped to around 2,000. The population of the town of Dornoch itself in 1939 was a mere 725.

Dornoch branch were Drummond 0-4-4Ts Nos.15051 and 15053. A visitor to the line in the summer of 1937 reported in the *Railway Observer* that *'...No.15053 works the Dornoch Light Railway; it was observed, neatly shedded, in the evening, and on the 9.10am train the next morning. According to the engine crew, this little machine has its boiler washed out once a fortnight, and goes to Inverness about every four months'.*

It has been stated elsewhere that, at some time during the LMSR period, a through sleeper was introduced between Dornoch and London, but was taken off after only a short period due to lack of patronage. Unfortunately, we have been unable to confirm or refute that unlikely sounding episode in the Dornoch branch's life. *(If any reader has information about the 'Dornoch Sleeper', we would be very interested to hear – Ed.)*

The public timetables for March 1940 listed three trains each way (weekdays only), but by November 1946 there were only two each way:
From Dornoch: 10.40am; 1.10pm
From The Mound: 11.50am; 2.00pm

The connections were:
• The 10.40am ex-Dornoch and 11.50am ex-The Mound connected with the 8.25am Wick-Inverness
• The 1.10pm ex-Dornoch and the 2.00pm ex-The Mound connected with the 10.40am Inverness-Wick.

The journey times of the branch trains were still in the region of 25-30 minutes, and it was still the usual practice to run mixed trains; the mainstays of the freight traffic were fish and livestock (outwards) and coal (inwards). By this time (1946), the two regular branch engines, Nos.15051 and 15053, were the only two survivors of their class; of the other two,

British Railways
In January 1948, the Dornoch branch duly became part of the Scottish Region of British Railways. The little engine shed at Dornoch formally became a sub-shed of Helmsdale which was given 'parent' status and subsequently coded 60C.

A visitor to the Dornoch branch on 15 May of that year reported that No.15051 – stated to be '...in filthy condition' – was in action on the line; it was also reported that, as the 10.40am ex-Inverness was running very late, the 2.00pm from The Mound had to held for some 90 minutes. On the same day, the other 0-4-4T, No.15053, was observed dead at Helmsdale shed. A return visit in October reported: *'...the situation at Dornoch is most critical as, during September, No.15053 had dropped her grate whilst on a train, and was laid off in the mid-road in Dornoch station, where she was still to be*

The exterior of Dornoch station, 30 July 1952. When the station opened in 1902 it had a bookshop run by a Mr.Gillespie. The station building was described as having a 'piend' roof – this is an old Scottish word for hipped. The building itself is now preserved. **PHOTOGRAPH: F.W.SHUTTLEWORTH**

A visit to Dornoch

The following is the late George Robin's account of a trip on the Dornoch branch in early part of July 1950. This account was part of a lengthy article which appeared in the Highland Railway Journal *(the magazine of the Highland Railway Society); this extract is reproduced by kind permission of Mr.Keith Fenwick, the editor of the Journal.*

George Robin's day started at Inverness where he joined the 7.00am train to Wick; it comprised nine corridors, a restaurant car and a vestibule for 'overflow', and was hauled by Black Five No.44961. He recalls that: '...on arrival at The Mound, it was to give the impression that the old Sutherland Railway (Bonar Bridge to Golspie) had been as sparing as possible with its limited capital. To my surprise, this station had one long and narrow platform on the right-hand side of the track, fairly straight at the southern end, but curving sharply away towards the water at the northern extremity. The station house was fairly substantial, much more so than at Rogart, while opposite the platform was a passing loop, off which led the scanty siding accommodation.

I noticed that the Light Railway came up on a 1 in 45 grade off the embankment, while the platform was on a lower level than the main line one. The junction was at the south end of the layout. Thus I was now half way to Wick, having travelled 80 miles from Inverness, and once the platform work was completed 44961 drew her train right forward, and as the right-hand curve mentioned above immediately becomes reverse and round a rock cutting, the driver must have had his mark for stopping before shunting the diner and vestibule carriage into a siding beside one of yon stinking gas tanks. The train left here 1½ minutes late for the barren wastes, while I had about 90 minutes to see around. I asked to have my case kept in the station office, and the station master just said "Put it down here and nobody will touch it". He told me that he came from Hamilton, and had got this isolated job easily. He appeared to me to be only about thirty years of age.

I was feeling a bit peckish now and felt the desire for a cup of coffee. I asked him where to go, but was told quite politely that there was no place within miles. However, he did give me permission to walk down the branch as far as the Mound embankment, situated just beyond the points, to get a photo of the train on it. That was OK in itself, but the line curved sharply and on the inside of the curve was a fine telegraph pole which would come right to the centre of the best exposure. Try as I might, I could not get in the arches across the road and the river (or perhaps a narrow neck of Loch Fleet) without an upright of some kind blotting out something more interesting. Then on the top of that there was a perfect plague of very large flies – may have been bluebottles – buzzing around and I could not shake them off either. I was dead scared that one would fly past the lens at the crucial moment because every now and then they were all that I could see through the view-finder. So after getting a good site and wandering around a little I at last saw the exhaust steam of the wee train meandering along the shore across Loch Fleet. Slowly but surely it approached, and I was soon able to see that it was mixed. At last it stopped at Cambusavie Halt, and I heard it leave and saw it appear in full view on the embankment. I am glad to say that my photo came out OK after all as I snapped the wee Highland 0-4-4 tank, looking as Highland as possible, as she came off the earthwork with her Stanier brake third composite and seven assorted goods vehicles and brake van. 55051 was the number today, and I understand that she and 55053 run alternate weeks on this run, the spare engine being kept at Helmsdale.

The early morning train from Wick and Thurso provided the next excitement as she arrived and departed behind 5P 44789. The wee tankie, 55051, now had the job of coupling on to the diners and attaching them to the rear of the up main line train. More photos. I also managed quite a few of 55051 and the station and the branch platform. As the branch grade is 1 in 250 at the platform, the Dornoch end is very much lower down than the main line one which rises in the same direction; consequently, steps down are required, while a dilapidated fence keeps passengers from breaking their necks. At one time I went back to the stationhouse for another spool for my camera, but on finding nobody there I just went in, and at the same time noticed that the safe was lying wide open!

55051 had disposed of her four covered and three open wagons, and the 11.50 branch train to Dornoch consisted only of the one coach with a few passengers, many churns of milk and the wee Highland tank.

Now this was a light railway, and I was to find out that the driver knew that. We went quite merrily down the 1 in 45 and crossed the bridges on to the embankment. Here the main road to Dornoch ran along parallel to us, though we fell to a lower level and, by means of a level crossing on the curve, we crossed the road and took to the shores of the Loch. Only 1¼ miles from the Junction we passed Cambusavie platform; it had the two Highland stop signals and the one for our direction was off. The tides, I expect, would be stopped by the embankment, and we were now on a sandy shore, as we ran along a lightly constructed track near what I took to be a disused road. However, I think it was once the main road, but I saw signs later of a better construction, and I think that this old one must have been left... *continued opposite...*

seen on 9th October, very rusty – this condition was painfully obvious to any passenger or passer-by. No.15051 was therefore carrying on single-handed, with the condition of one of the driving axleboxes causing grave doubts as it was running warm and shedding white metal'.

No.15053 was later taken to St.Rollox for repair; it emerged in January 1949, not only in good mechanical health, but also sporting BRITISH RAILWAYS lettering on its tanks and its new BR number, 55053. The other Dornoch regular, No.15051, was dispatched to St.Rollox soon after, and emerged in April as BR No.55051.

It remained the standard practice for one of the two 0-4-4Ts to be in use and the other kept as a spare, usually at Helmsdale. However, on 6 October 1952 No.55051 was noted at Inverness, working as the carriage and wagon shunter; apparently it had been sent down from Helmsdale for a routine boiler examination, and was merely earning its keep at Inverness before being sent back to Helmsdale the following day. A visitor to the area on 1 July 1953 reported that No.55053 was on the Dornoch branch and No.55051 was on shed at Helmsdale. A return visit on 6 October of that year revealed that No.55053 was once again the branch engine, but on this occasion No.55051 was undertaking a little light shunting at Helmsdale.

In the early 1950s there was a change in the mode of working the Dornoch branch, the opening and closing of the six sets of level crossing gates along the route now being undertaken by the guard of the train. This, of course, all took time, and the journey times were consequently increased to 43 minutes (down) and 46 minutes (up) for the 7¾ miles. However, there were only two trains each way to be affected; the timetables for the summer of 1954 list:

From Dornoch: 10.25am; 1.00pm
From The Mound: 11.55am; 2.05pm

The connections were:
• The 10.25am ex-Dornoch and the 11.55am ex-The Mound connected with the 8.35am Wick-Inverness
• The 1.00pm ex-Dornoch and the 2.05pm ex-The Mound connected with 10.40am Inverness-Wick.

Of those main line connections, the 8.35am from Wick was advertised in the public timetables as having a restaurant car from The Mound to Inverness. The car had arrived at The Mound on the 6.40am ex-Inverness (scheduled arrival at The Mound at 9.52am) and was taken off at there and placed in a siding to await attachment to the southbound train from Wick to Inverness; this was due at The Mound at 11.31am. This transfer of the restaurant car at The Mound was a long-standing practice.

In the early 1950s the platform face at Dornoch was renewed and the station buildings repainted, the platforms at Skelbo and Embo rebuilt, and the branch itself relaid with 60ft rails. It was considered in some circles that the laying of new rails would pave the way for the regular use of ex-Caledonian 2P 0-4-4Ts on the line. However, that was not to happen –

continued from previous page...

...to serve intermediate points. Shortly, larger boulders and very large patches of seaweed almost blotted out the sand on the shore and, after seeing some old stone piers, or jetties, on the loch side, we drew up at Skelbo platform, 3¾ miles on our journey. The platform just held our coach with enough room left for a four-wheeled van. It was placed on the right hand or landward side of the line and one passenger got out. Why, I don't know, as all that I could see was isolation. Onwards we struck grades of 1 in 50, and the countryside became more gorse covered now, while the art of driving on a light railway seemed to be that of keeping a steady 15mph up and down the ever changing steep grades of the switchback. Soon we came upon a long straight stretch, mostly at 1 in 50 up, and what a miserable preamble it was.

At the top here was Embo (5½ miles) and this was quite a large place, but also with a single platform, though on the left side this time, while there was quite a big yard at the Dornoch end. Three folk got in here. Shortly after leaving, a golf course appeared on the inland side, while the seashore sported a fine long, though narrow, stretch of lovely golden sand. We were now on a long straight descent, but right at the foot and just round a very sharp bend was a level crossing with gates, a keeper and the usual signal in each direction for protecting such existences. Immediately, a very sharp reverse curve (to the right) took us into the station area of the terminus. The large wooden faced platform was on the left side, and was of remarkable length. There was no signal box and no turntable, but there was a fair sized yard with a covered-in goods shed and a small engine shed, while provision was made for watering engines. We arrived about seven minutes late and I noticed that the station platform was quite a "market", people having free access to the shop or two on it. I took a photo here. I do not know how to account for my excitement here, but both this exposure and one that I took before leaving were "double-exposured" with ones at the Mound. Although I was able to duplicate the Mound ones later on, I did not have the chance to do the same with the photos at Dornoch. Still, I cannot be lucky every time, though I should be more careful.

I had only one hour at Dornoch and thought it fitting to get the inner man filled again as I had had nothing since my 6.15am breakfast at Inverness, and I had no idea where I would get my tea. I chanced upon the burnt-out ruins of the "Sutherland Arms Hotel" upon following some signposts, but they had an annexe which served up a very fine lunch. As a matter of fact, it was quite the meal of this outing, and not having any time to explore the town (what a real pity) I made for the station once again. Dornoch station was situated on a fringe, but as far as I could see the track could not really have economically been brought nearer to the town centre. I had a chat with the driver who told me that he and his mate were the only crew this summer. Last summer (1949) an afternoon trip was run and this necessitated a crew being brought up from Inverness to live in digs and did not pay. The driver was definitely of the opinion that as things were worked at present that the branch was paying. It may or it may not, but it was good hearing.

The trip back to the main line was uneventful. A lot of sundries were picked up at Embo and another single passenger got out at Skelbo; while as we passed Cambusavie Halt, I noticed that the signals had not been altered since we passed earlier, and that the one which was "off" was the arm for the Dornoch direction. It is interesting to note that the signals at this halt were of the Upper Quadrant type, while The Mound also had been re-signalled with this modern tone. So once more I could say that I had travelled over another interesting byway, and once more could I say that I had travelled behind an engine of the old Highland Railway.

At The Mound, there was little for me to do except hang around for the Wick train to come along in about half an hours time. However, I made the unfortunate discovery that I had been careless with my camera, and had made a double exposure of both the snaps at Dornoch station. By good luck, I was now able to repeat the misses at The Mound. The day was still dullish with low cloud, but as the sun was casting no shadow it made photographing all the easier, as I could choose either side of the locomotives. The main line train was late in arriving behind yet another 5P 4-6-0, 44798, and consisted of mail van, diner, four corridors for Wick and three for Thurso, and so tared at a little short of 300 tons. I managed an empty seat in the Thurso section, but must say that the train was well filled...'.

at least, not permanently – and so Nos.55051 and 55053 soldiered on.

A visitor to Inverness on the evening of Wednesday 6 July 1955 observed No.55053 arriving at the shed for its routine wash-out. It was apparently due to return to Helmsdale on Friday 8th, departing light engine from Inverness at 5.00am. While No.55053 was away from Helmsdale, the Dornoch branch was worked by No.55051 or, occasionally, Helmsdale's spare engine, Caley 0-4-4T No.55162. As for No.55051, it was reported in July 1955 that it was due to be sent to St.Rollox for repair, but the state of its boiler was so bad that a one-way trip to Kilmarnock seemed to be a realistic alternative. Later in July 1955 No.55053 went to St.Rollox for repair and, when it emerged, it sported a fully-lined BR livery. It was the only ex-Highland engine ever to receive the full BR passenger livery.

At this time, the Dornoch branch train comprised a corridor brake composite together with a van for parcels. It appears that the passenger coach was changed fairly frequently – in other words, there was not a designated branch coach. One of the two daily trains in each direction was mixed, and usually had a handful of vans attached behind the coach.

In April 1956 No.55051 was finally laid up. It was formally withdrawn three months later. This left No.55053 to soldier on alone on the Dornoch branch, with 2P No.55236 being available as cover, if and when required. As a result of the relaying of the Dornoch branch a few years earlier, in June 1956 the line's axle-weight limit was officially increased to 14 tons. This permitted the use of BR or ex-LMSR 'Class 2' 2-6-0s on the branch; at least, that was the theory – in practice, no Class 2s were allocated to the Far North, the nearest shed with a representation being Keith, which was no less than 150 miles away.

The quest for alternative forms of motive power on the branch suddenly took on considerable urgency on 16 November 1956. While on a routine branch working – one corridor coach and a couple of fish vans – the locomotive's leading coupled axle broke. One wheel parted company from the axle and ran along the ballast but, fortunately, the engine and train remained on the rails and nobody was hurt. No.55053 was taken to Lochgorm Works to await a decision as to its future. Given that its classmate, No.55051, had been cut up with indecent haste sixteen months earlier, there was no source of spare parts and so the only option for No.55053 was withdrawal. This was formally effected during the week ending 12 January 1957. No.55053 had claimed the distinction of being the last ex-Highland engine in BR service; it had considerably outlived the actuarial estimate of 25 years!

To temporarily fill the void on the Dornoch branch, Standard Class 2 2-6-0 No.78052 was hastily transferred to Inverness, with 2P 0-4-4T No.55236 retained as cover. However, a permanent replacement for No.55053 was soon identified, and it came in a very unexpected guise. It was Western Region 16XX class 0-6-0PT No.1646, which left its home at Croes Newydd on 7 February 1957 (being incorporated into a goods train) and arrived at Helmsdale four days later. No.1646 proved to be very well

The Mound and Dornoch — **Table 119**

WEEKDAYS ONLY

Mls		a.m.	..	..	a.m.	..	..		a.m.	..	..	p.m	..	..	..
..	117 Inverness .... lev.	6 40	..	..	1040	..	..	Dornoch .... lev.	1025	..	..	1 0	..	..	..
..	The Mound	11̄55	..	..	2 p 5	..	..	Embo	1033	..	..	1 8	..	..	..
1¼	Cambusavie Platform	12A4	..	..	2A14	..	..	Skelbo	1045	..	..	1 20	..	..	..
3¾	Skelbo	1217	..	..	2 27	..	..	Cambusavie Platform	11A0	..	..	1A35	..	..	..
5½	Embo	1226	..	..	2 36	..	..	The Mound	1111	..	..	1 46	..	..	..
7¾	Dornoch ...... arr.	1238	..	..	2 48	..	..	117 Inverness .... arr.	2 40	.	..	..	..	..	..

Scottish Region public timetable, 14 June to 19 September 1952.

No.55053 and its mixed train (the 2.05pm from The Mound) approach Dornoch on 1 October 1953. The train has just negoti-ated the level crossing 20 chains (¼ mile) short of the terminus. The coach is a flush-sided ex-LMSR 62ft vehicle; it appears to be one of those which had been built at Wolverton between 1935 and 1938. There seemed to be no preference as to which way round the coaches faced on the branch – in some photographs the brake end is nearest the terminus while, in others, it is nearest The Mound. PHOTOGRAPH: A.B.FLETCHER

suited to the Dornoch branch and so, in July 1958, another of the class, No.1649, was also dispatched to Helmsdale. It had previously been allocated to St.Philip's Marsh shed in Bristol. The use of these two 16XXs in the Far North prompted the suggestion that, with others of the class allocated to sheds in Cornwall, this dis-persal of a class was almost certainly a peacetime record.

The pannier tanks had only a short time to become accustomed to their new surroundings. By the early part of 1960, proposals to close twenty of the interme-diate stations between Inverness and

Wick looked like becoming reality. One of the stations earmarked for closure was The Mound, and this would, of course, render the Dornoch branch trains redun-dant. The closure of The Mound and the Dornoch branch was effected on Monday 13 June 1960 but, in the absence of Sun-day services, the last public passenger trains ran on Saturday 11th. The branch engine on the 'last day' was No.1649. The morning return trip consisted of the cus-tomary single coach plus a handful of freight vans, but for the second (and fi-nal) trip three corridor coaches were pro-vided. After the final arrival at Dornoch,

No.1649 had to clear the goods vans from the station yard as well as returning the empty coaching stock.

The closure of the Dornoch branch had not been confirmed until fairly late in the day; clearly, it had not been confirmed when the Scottish Region had printed its public timetables for the summer of 1960, as the branch services (all two of them!) were listed in the timetable which came into force on 13 June of that year. The two Pannier Tanks remained in the area un-til their withdrawal in December 1962. Their work included station piloting at Dingwall.

The three intermediate stations on the Dornoch branch were sel-dom photographed, and so this picture of Embo is something of a rarity. It was taken on 8 June 1960 and looks south towards Dornoch. As noted in the text, the station platform was rebuilt in the early 1950s. PHOTOGRAPH: LYNDON W.ROWE

Having left The Mound station, No.55051 crosses The Mound itself – this is the causeway over the River Fleet – with a mixed train for Dornoch on 30 July 1952. Photographer Tim Shuttleworth recalls that he and his brother were the only passengers to board the train at The Mound; the train was not required to stop at Cambusavie as no passengers wished to board or alight there, but two or three passengers joined at Skelbo and Embo. After arrival at Dornoch the engine undertook a little shunting then returned to the platform as if to depart with the passenger coach; however, there were no more trains that day, so Messrs. Shuttleworth & Shuttleworth had to return to The Mound by bus. PHOTOGRAPH: F.W.SHUTTLEWORTH

The Dornoch branch train, with No.55051 in charge, approaches The Mound on 23 April 1952 – that year seemed to be a popular one with photographers! PHOTOGRAPH: H.C.CASSERLEY

Clearly, the station at The Mound did not serve a bustling centre of population. On 23 April 1952 No.55051 waits to depart from the somewhat isolated station with the 11.55am to Dornoch. The coach is brake corridor compo SC6755M, one of a batch of twenty-five 60ft coaches built at Wolverton in 1930. It was not originally flush-sided – rebuilding took place *circa* 1940 when it received 'Period III' panels and deep window ventilators. PHOTOGRAPH: H.C.CASSERLEY

The line was lifted in 1962. Many of the level crossing cottages are still in use as private dwellings, but the site of the junction at The Mound is now overgrown, with no reason for trains to stop there. The A9 trunk road has nowadays cut the distance between, say, Tain and Dornoch to 9 miles – it was five times as long by rail! Much anger was created in Scotland in the early 1990s by the Government's refusal to allow a diverted Highland main line to cross Dornoch Firth with the road on the new bridge. Any researcher wishing to examine the official SRO file on the controversy will find that it is closed to 2016; so we must wait until then to grasp the Transport Minister's reason for refusing to allow the Far North line to gain a new lease of life, and for trains to once again run into the pleasant town of Dornoch.

Research note: Papers relating to the Dornoch Light (BR/DLR/1/1) and Highland Railways have been researched at the Scottish Record Office, whose staff are thanked for their helpfulness. An interest-

This splendid view of the branch platform at The Mound includes a nice array of wicker hampers, milk churns and a hand cart, and could easily be a period piece from the 1920s or 1930s. It was, however, taken on 30 July 1952. The main line platform is behind the railings on the left. PHOTOGRAPH: F.W.SHUTTLEWORTH

Returning to Dornoch, this view of the station shows the goods shed in the spacious yard. No.55051 waits with the 1.15pm to Dornoch on 23 April 1952. PHOTOGRAPH: R.M.CASSERLEY

ing booklet exclusively describing the line was written and published by Barry C. Turner in 1987 (ISBN 09513358 04). Some of the locomotive information was gleaned from Highland Railway Locomotives *(Cormack & Stevenson – RCTS, 1988), while other information was taken from contemporary railway magazines, notably the* Railway Observer.

Thanks are also due to Mr. Keith Fenwick, the editor of The Highland Railway Journal *(the magazine of the Highland Railway Society), for granting permission to use extracts from George Robin's articles which appeared in the Journal. For details of membership of the Highland Railway Society, contact Mr. Don Massey, 17 Wellyards Close, Weston, Stafford ST18 0JWE (we imagine an s.a.e. would be regarded as a common courtesy).*

Thanks also to Messrs. Tim Shuttleworth and John Edgington for information about the coaching stock, to Mr. Bryan L. Wilson for information about The Mound signal box, and to Mr. Lyndon W. Rowe for details of his visit to the line in June 1960.

No.55051 shunts at the north-west end of The Mound station on 30 July 1952. The photographer is standing on the end of the branch platform – we are looking along the main line in the direction of Rogart (or Inverness, if you prefer) – and the engine appears to have picked up wagons from the dead-end sidings adjacent to the main line. The mixed train now complete, it is being hauled back to the branch platform ready for the return trip to Dornoch. A gas tank wagon stands on the siding to the right of the main line. The bridge under which the train is passing carries the Dornoch-Golspie main road (part of which is now incorporated in the A9) near its junction with the road from Lairg. The bridge was built in 1939 to replace an older structure; the abutments of the old bridge can be seen in front of those of the new one. PHOTOGRAPH: F.W.SHUTTLEWORTH

A very fine portrait of the smartly lined No.55053 at Inverness shed in 1956. PHOTOGRAPH: THE TRANSPORT TREASURY

After breaking an axle and losing a wheel while in service, No.55053 was dispatched to Lochgorm Works at Inverness pending a decision as to its fate. The decision – the somewhat inevitable one – was withdrawal. It was photographed at Lochgorm on 24 June 1957 awaiting removal to Kilmarnock for scrap. PHOTOGRAPH: THE TRANSPORT TREASURY

The unexpected replacements for the Highland 0-4-4Ts were Western Region 0-6-0PTs. The second of the pair to arrive in the Far North was No.1649, which was photographed at Dornoch on Wednesday 8 June 1960 (the last week of services) preparing to depart with the 1.00pm to The Mound. The tower in the background is that of Dornoch Cathedral. PHOTO-GRAPH: LYNDON W.ROWE

The first of the WR 16XXs to reach Scotland was No.1646. It was photographed sometime shortly after its arrival in February 1957 hauling a mixed train from Dornoch towards The Mound. The coach is SC6742M, another of the Wolverton-built 60ft coaches of 1930 which had been rebuilt with flush sides *circa* 1940. PHOTOGRAPH: C.LAWSON KERR

No.1646 crosses the viaduct over the River Fleet some time in February 1957. PHOTOGRAPH: C.LAWSON KERR

No.1649 runs round the branch train at The Mound on 8 June 1960. On the opposite side of the main line is the handsome signal box – this was typical of Highland 'boxes of 1900 onwards, having a brick base but retaining the old Highland-style timber batten end gable. PHOTOGRAPH: LYNDON W.ROWE

Having run round the train, No.1649 rejoins the platform road and is about to couple up again. The structure on the right is the water tank. PHOTOGRAPH: LYNDON W.ROWE

Both of the Dornoch pannier tanks, Nos.1646 and 1649, simmer at The Mound on 8 June 1960 – this was three days before the cessation of services. Photographer Lyndon Rowe informs us that he had travelled that morning from Helmsdale to The Mound on the 8.35am from Wick, and both pannier tanks were there on his arrival. No.1649 took him to Dornoch on the 11.55am and returned with the 1.00pm to The Mound. By this time No.1646 had vanished from the scene, possibly back to Helmsdale shed. The reason for the two panniers having been at The Mound in the morning is a bit of a mystery; the photographs shows a distinct difference in the level of coal in their bunkers, and this could be taken to suggest that the branch engine was being changed. However, as far as we are aware, engine changes were undertaken at weekends. Hmmm… Putting this matter to one side, this picture also gives a good view of the other end of the signal box – the 'panelled' brick base, slate roof and plain bargeboards are typical of Highland 'boxes of the 1900s, though the roof has lost the finials which once adorned it. The high outcrop in the distance is part of Mound Rock. PHOTOGRAPH: LYNDON W.ROWE

And finally...

Photograph by W.J.Ford

For the last four and a half years or so RAILWAY BYLINES has been 'spreading the word', as it were, about industrial railways. We have been trying to show that there was more to Britain's railway heritage – much, much more – than Black Fives, Bulleid Pacifics and big main-line stations. The industrial scene offered a wonderful alternative to all that 'main line' stuff; there was also oodles of variety to be found, as each industrial system had very distinct characteristics of its own. Furthermore, if one knew where to look, there was plenty of scope for taking first-rate photographs. This little gem was taken on the Finedon Quarries 3ft 3in gauge system just to the north-east of Wellingborough in Northamptonshire. One of the Peckett 0-6-0STs is working hard, bringing six well-loaded wagons of ironstone from the quarries.